When Should the Watchdogs Bark?

★ ★ ★ ★ ★ ★ ★ ★ ★ ★ ★ ★ ★

Media Coverage
of the
Clinton Scandals

When Should the Watchdogs Bark?

* * * * * * * * * * *

Media Coverage of the Clinton Scandals

Larry J. Sabato
&
S. Robert Lichter

Center for Media and Public Affairs
Washington, DC

Copyright © 1994 by the
Center for Media and Public Affairs
Washington, D.C.

University Press of America,® Inc.
4720 Boston Way
Lanham, Maryland 20706

3 Henrietta Street
London WC2E 8LU England

Copublished by arrangement with the
Center for Media and Public Affairs

Library of Congress Catalog Card Number: 94-69209

ISBN 0-9643877-0-0

1 3 5 7 9 10 8 6 4 2

First Edition

TABLE OF CONTENTS

INTRODUCTION

The Clinton administration has been battered by several personal scandal stories that have dogged the president throughout his term of office. These include the Clintons' Whitewater investments (and associated financial and political stories), Troopergate (accusations of philandering by then-Governor Clinton made by his Arkansas state trooper guards), and Paula Corbin Jones's claims of sexual harassment against Mr. Clinton.

The president and his supporters have blamed the news media for this sour turn of events. They complain that journalists have gone the extra mile to "dig up dirt" about Mr. Clinton and have given wide circulation to unfounded charges. Indeed, it *is* unusual for campaign issues to be recycled and given such prominence by the press, especially so early in a presidency.

Why have events unfolded in this fashion? How did the news media come to treat so harshly a politician once highly esteemed by many leading journalists? Are the president's complaints of unfair coverage justified? Alternatively, as his critics charge, has the media actually been too hesitant to cover legitimate issues relating to this president's private life? Finally, can the media treatment of this president's travails provide valuable lessons about the strengths and weaknesses of scandal coverage that are applicable to future circumstances?

One conclusion is obvious from the outset: The character issue still vexes the press. Journalists and news organizations are undeniably uncomfortable with it, certain that people are interested in the subject but wishing it would just go away. ***But it won't go away***. The deepening public concern about moral decline, and the resurgence of cultural values in political debate, guarantee that the very questions at the heart of Bill Clinton's "character problems" will arise again and again.

Yet the news media seemingly have learned little since 1987, when a *Washington Post* reporter asked presidential candidate Gary Hart whether he had ever committed adultery. Sophistication in character coverage today is rare, and its absence has been noted anew as the Clinton scandals have unfolded. Will the media ever get it right? Do they even want to do so? What can be learned on this score from the news coverage of Whitewater, Troopergate, and Paula Jones? This study will draw some distinctions among private life stories that might help the press get it right... next time.

In conducting the study, members of the research team interviewed thirty-six major media journalists, most of whom had been directly involved in covering one or more of the Clinton scandal stories. (They are listed in an appendix on p. 123.) Thirteen of the interviewees were broadcast journalists, while twenty-three were print reporters. Twenty-four were on-air correspondents or by-lined reporters; twelve were editors, producers, or news executives with supervisory control over the stories being studied.

All direct quotations in the text, unless otherwise specifically attributed, were drawn from the interviews. About two-thirds of the interviewees agreed to go on-the-record for all or almost all of their comments. The others gave their remarks completely off-the-record or on background. Thus, some of the comments we quote are necessarily unidentified. Some requested prior approval of any comment we chose to quote in this report, and all such requests were of course granted.

Unless the interviewee insisted otherwise, every session was tape recorded, and the tapes have been preserved. Beyond the thirty-six listed interviewees, five more reporters and editors contributed information and background quotations but would not permit their names to be cited, even in the appendix. We appreciate the time, cooperation, and candor of everyone interviewed for this study.

In addition to interviewing journalists, we examined the actual major media coverage of scandal allegations against Mr. Clinton. To assess the television coverage, we relied on the Center for Media and Public Affairs' systematic content analysis of all ABC, CBS, and NBC evening news shows broadcast from November 1, 1993 to August 15, 1994. In all, 311 TV stories about Whitewater, Troopergate, and Paula Jones were examined for the statistical portions of this study. This part of the study was conducted under the able direction of CMPA's Political Studies Director, Richard Noyes.

Supplementing the television research was a qualitative analysis of all print stories relating to the three scandals that appeared in the *New York Times, Washington Post, Los Angeles Times, Washington Times, Time, Newsweek,* and *U. S. News & World Report* over the same time period. All together, 1,235 print stories were analyzed, 1,082 from the newspapers and 153 from the newsmagazines.

Only stories where the content was **substantially** devoted to one or more of the scandals were included; mere scandal mentions in articles about other subjects, as well as very brief items (such as *Newsweek*'s CW column) and all editorials and op-ed pieces, were excluded from the study.

One stylistic matter should be clarified at the outset: Throughout this manuscript, terms like "scandal" and "scandal story" refer to the topical focus of the allegations about Mr. Clinton's behavior. They are not intended to prejudge the truth or falsity of these allegations.

This study benefited from the assistance of numerous individuals during its design, execution, and publication. At the Center for Media and Public Affairs, Linda Lichter helped develop the coding system. Mary Carroll Gunning assisted in CMPA's research and provided graphics, layout, and composition.   Michelle Fernandez helped prepare the manuscript for publication.   John Sheehan assisted with manuscript revisions and co-ordinated CMPA's publication of this book.

Many of the interviews and much of the newspaper research, data-gathering, and report drafting, were done by graduate student Thomas Hetlage and undergraduate student David Kaefer of the University of Virginia.   The hard work and dedication of these outstanding young scholars has been much appreciated and is gratefully acknowledged.   This study could not have been completed without them, and it has been greatly enriched by their creative enterprise.

Larry J. Sabato
University of Virginia

S. Robert Lichter
Center for Media and Public Affairs

October 1994

- ONE -

News Coverage of the Clinton Scandals: An Overview

The Clinton administration has been buffeted by stories about the president's financial and personal activities, primarily while he was governor of Arkansas. On the business end of Mr. Clinton's Arkansas life have been the Whitewater allegations. Questions have been raised about (1) Bill and Hillary Clinton's losses from Whitewater Development Corporation; (2) Whitewater's connection to Madison Guaranty, a failed savings and loan that was operated by James McDougal, the Clintons' Whitewater co-investor; and (3) other aspects of the Clintons' involvement in the closely interwoven political, business, and legal circles of Little Rock. Subsequently, the Clinton administration's handling of the investigation into Whitewater has also come under scrutiny.

Charges about the president's past have not been limited to dry financial issues. The president has also faced a variety of allegations involving his personal life while governor. In late 1993, four Arkansas state troopers who had worked on then-Governor Clinton's security detail publicly accused him of rampant womanizing and misuse of state employees. In February 1994, Paula Corbin Jones, a former employee of a state agency in Arkansas, accused President Clinton of sexual harrassment during a Little Rock hotel room encounter in 1991. Several months later, Jones filed a $700,000 federal lawsuit against the president, claiming a violation of her civil rights.

The role of the media has always been fundamental in the course of political scandals, and President Clinton's alleged wrong-doings are no exception. Journalists and media critics alike have repeatedly reevaluated the press's role in these affairs, questioning both the degree to which the spotlight should shine on such scandals and what issues are fair game.

The key difference between the president's personal controversies and his financial problems involves the media's view of the legitimacy of the subject matter. Whitewater represents a fairly typical political scandal, involving allegations about financial dealings and the possible misuse of official power to unduly influence them. The decision to publish or broadcast such a story involves relatively little journalistic handwringing, and the public relevance of these issues is widely accepted. The Troopergate and Paula Jones incidents represent a less traditional form of scandal that has increasingly created difficult dilemmas for journalists. Is a president's personal life fair game for coverage? Are transgressions in this arena relevant to an individual's performance in office? Where should the press draw the line between the public's "right to know" and a violation of a politician's legitimate privacy rights?

The contrast between the media's approaches in these two different kinds of scandals makes for compelling study. In essence, Whitewater represents the "control" for the comparison. This characterization by no means excuses the disturbing excesses in Whitewater coverage, from occasional absurd comparisons with Watergate to the consequent eclipsing of far more important domestic and foreign policy issues. [See the damning indictment of the press's Whitewater obsession in Thomas E. Patterson's most recent edition of *Out of Order* (New York: Vintage, 1994), pp. 243-250.]

For better or worse, the press treatment of Whitewater has been that of a traditional feeding frenzy. Troopergate and Paula Jones are in a newer and separate category of character controversies. The ways in which the coverage of these personal scandals adhered to or veered away from the norm of the Whitewater frenzy is revealing — not just for these individual scandals but also for the press corp's standards in the 1990s.

The Chronology of Coverage

The Whitewater story first surfaced nationally during the 1992 campaign. That March the *New York Times* reported that the Clintons had been co-investors in Whitewater Development Corporation along with James McDougal. The primary allegation in the story was that, while the Clintons were fifty percent owners of Whitewater, they had invested thousands less in the land deal than James McDougal and his wife Susan. The Clinton campaign denied any wrongdoing and assigned Denver attorney James Lyons the task of preparing a report on the Clintons' investment. Lyons concluded that the Clintons had lost approximately $69,000 on Whitewater. After the Lyons report, the complex story virtually disappeared for the balance of the campaign, lost in a welter of primaries and sexier issues.

The matter reemerged in the fall of 1993. The *Washington Post* reported on October 31 that the Resolution Trust Corporation had asked the Justice Department to probe James McDougal for the possible misuse of depositor funds from his S&L, Madison Guaranty. A trickle of stories appeared in the mainstream press during November and early December, documenting the Clintons' relationship with McDougal. These stories and McDougal's 1985 role in helping retire Governor Clinton's substantial personal debt from the previous year's gubernatorial campaign.

Serious allegations against the president by former judge David Hale also began to appear in print and over the airwaves. Hale (who was under indictment for the fraudulent use of loans backed by the Small Business Administration) alleged that Clinton had encouraged him to make a $300,000 SBA-sponsored loan to Susan McDougal so that some of the money could go into the financially strapped Whitewater Corporation. As it happened, $120,000 of the loan did go to Whitewater, although the president said that he did not recollect meeting Hale. In April 1994,

Hale entered into a plea agreement with then-special counsel Robert Fiske. Hale pled guilty to a single felony count of fraud in exchange for his testimony regarding Whitewater.

This trickle of coverage turned into a flood in the third week of December. Over the weekend before Christmas, the press began publishing stories about a missing Whitewater file that had been in the office of Associate White House Counsel Vincent Foster when he committed suicide in July 1993. On December 20, the *Washington Times* reported that the file had been secretly removed during a search of the office hours after Foster's death. This story has been widely credited with generating an avalanche of attention to Whitewater-related subjects.

Over the next several weeks pressure grew on Capitol Hill and elsewhere for the appointment of a special counsel. The president rejected such calls until mid-January, when he finally relented. On January 20, Attorney General Janet Reno named attorney Robert Fiske as the special counsel for Whitewater. Much of the media focus during this period was on congressional reaction and the political ramifications of the emerging scandal.

Throughout the spring of 1994, the press created many Whitewater tributaries that branched out into auxiliary areas. Among these were the shredding of documents at Little Rock's Rose Law Firm, the former employer of Hillary Rodham Clinton and Vincent Foster; improper contacts between Treasury officials and the White House; and a phone call from White House aide George Stephanopoulos to the Treasury Department questioning the hiring of a former Republican-appointed U.S. Attorney, Jay Stephens, to work on the RTC's investigation of Madison Guaranty. Most wildly speculative of the ancillary subjects were rumors suggesting that Foster's death was not a suicide.

In late March, the president held a prime-time news conference to answer Whitewater questions, at which he revised his losses on the land deal downward from $69,000 to $47,000. The Clintons' tax returns, released the following day, supported that figure. Also in March, the *New York Times* reported that Mrs.

Clinton had made nearly $100,000 in the commodities market in the late 1970s. Several weeks later, after a report in *Newsweek* inaccurately reported that Mrs. Clinton had put no money down on the deal, the White House released trading records showing that the First Lady had actually invested $1,000 to create the windfall.

The Whitewater frenzy calmed by late spring and remained fairly tranquil until July and August, when House and Senate hearings were held on the Washington part of the Whitewater story. While severely limited in scope and more an opportunity for partisan exchanges, the hearings eventually resulted in the resignation of Deputy Treasury Secretary Roger Altman and Treasury General Counsel Jean Hanson. Also in August, a panel of judges refused to name Robert Fiske as independent counsel, instead appointing Kenneth Starr, a former federal judge and solicitor general during the Bush administration.

Media coverage of Whitewater reached its crescendo in late February and early March of 1994. During that period, Whitewater stories regularly eclipsed issues such as health care and welfare reform in the battle for front-page headlines. Over the entire ten months we examined for this study, Whitewater generated 618 articles in three major newspapers (the *Washington Post, New York Times*, and *Los Angeles Times*). ABC's "World News Tonight" devoted virtually an entire newscast to the story in mid-February. *Time* magazine offered an ominous looking (and misleading) Oval Office photo of the president and Mr. Stephanopoulos on its cover, as the press coverage reached its peak in March. Moreover, in classic scandal reporting style, Whitewater became an omnipresent context for stories on the president's every move or decision: "Still hounded by questions over Whitewater, the president departed for Europe today... ."

By contrast, neither set of allegations about the president's personal life approached the quantity or tone of Whitewater coverage. The Troopergate story appeared briefly on the media's radar scope in late December 1993. Four Arkansas state troopers, who had served as bodyguards for Mr. Clinton while he was governor, claimed that he had used them to facilitate numerous extramarital trysts. In addition, two troopers alleged that the president had offered them federal jobs in September 1993 in exchange for their silence about his past.

The original stories appeared in the conservative *American Spectator* on December 20 and the *Los Angeles Times* the following day. (See Sidebar A, pp. 65-72.) Two of the troopers also gave interviews to CNN, which aired excerpts on December 19. The president called the accusations "outrageous," and the credibility of the troopers was called into question by the revelation, reported a few days later in the *New York Times*, that they had lied in a 1990 auto insurance case.

The media's attention to the story varied somewhat from outlet to outlet. Some news organizations, such as *U.S. News & World Report,* essentially ignored Troopergate altogether. Other outlets gave it more focus, but mainly through profiles of some of the actors (such as Cliff Jackson, the troopers' lawyer and a Clinton adversary), or through analyses of the press coverage. In essence, the entire story was basically dead within a single week.

The other character allegation that haunted the president was Paula Corbin Jones's claim of sexual harrassment. Jones originally leveled her explosive charge at a February 11, 1994 news conference at the Conservative Political Action Committee convention in Washington. According to Jones, Danny Ferguson, one of Clinton's Arkansas trooper bodyguards, had solicited her on behalf of the governor at a hotel in Little Rock. While she was working at a conference registration table for the Arkansas Industrial Development Commission, she alleged, Ferguson told her that the governor wanted to meet her, and he led her to a hotel room where Mr. Clinton was waiting. Once inside, said Jones, the governor attempted to kiss and touch her, exposed himself, and asked her to perform oral sex on him. She insisted that she rejected his advances and eventually left, at which point Clinton supposedly told her, "You are smart. Let's keep this between ourselves." At the news conference, Jones stated that she was seeking an apology and might file a lawsuit against Clinton.

The story reemerged in early May as Jones prepared to follow through on her threat. The president hired Robert Bennett, a high-powered Washington attorney, to defend him against the looming lawsuit. On May 6, Jones filed a $700,000 suit in federal court claiming that her civil rights had been violated. In addition to the emotional distress caused by the alleged event, Jones also said that she had been denied raises at work in the aftermath of the incident. Bennett later filed a brief claiming that a president is immune from civil suits while in office, an argument with which the Justice Department agreed in a separate brief.

Media coverage varied widely on the day of Jones' original CPAC press conference. Most news organizations made very limited mention of her allegations. A few, such as CBS, NBC and CNN, gave no attention at all to the accusations. The *Washington Post* did not run a story the following day, but it did initiate an extensive investigation. The *Post* ran a lengthy story on its finding several months later on May 5, the day after Robert Bennett's services were engaged. (See Sidebar B, pp.73-78.) The hiring of Bennett and the filing of the lawsuit brought the rest of the media into the story. All of the major news organizations reported on the suit, and many began a limited examination of the story, mostly of the personal history of Paula Jones. Subsequently, Jones would be interviewed on ABC's "Prime Time Live" by Sam Donaldson and on CNN by Judy Woodruff.

Thus, allegations of personal scandal against Mr. Clinton were barely covered by the mainstream media, in marked contrast to their Whitewater coverage. And in total, over the course of Mr. Clinton's presidency, scandal news of all types has accounted for only five percent of the administration's coverage on the network evening news broadcasts, according to a recent study conducted by the Center for Media and Public Affairs. [*Media Monitor* VIII (July/August 1994).] That is, only 240 out of 4,256

TV news stories broadcast from January 1993 through late June 1994 centered on scandal topics. Concerning President Clinton personally, nearly four out of five soundbites on television news (79 percent) were concerned with *policy* issues, compared to just six percent regarding *character* questions.

Additionally, Mr. Clinton's character was criticized by fewer news sources than his policy performance. While 56 percent of the sources quoted by the networks spoke unfavorably about Mr. Clinton's character, 64 percent of the cited sources criticized the president on policy matters. Even with Whitewater included, then, the broadcast media cannot really be accused of overdoing scandal coverage *as a whole.*

Structure of This Study

The media's handling of the Clinton scandals is addressed at length in Chapter Two. Our primary focus will be on the press coverage of the two personal scandals, with Whitewater — as mentioned earlier — serving as the "control" for comparative purposes. First, we will outline differences in the media's coverage of Troopergate and Paula Jones versus coverage of Whitewater. Disparities in the coverage of the scandals will be charted using both quantitative data and qualitative analysis. Among the questions we will seek to answer are these: Did the press require a higher standard of proof for the character scandals than for Whitewater stories? And were the primary accusers in the Troopergate and Paula Jones stories treated differently in the media than the major sources in Whitewater?

In Chapter Three, we discuss the reasons for differences in the coverage. Is the mainstream U.S. press generally uneasy about "sex stories," and if so, why? Did the media make clear distinctions between the purely sexual content of the stories, and alleged abuses of office that were related to the alleged sexual behavior? What justifications did the press have for avoiding the stories about the president's personal life, and were these justifications applied equally to the Whitewater coverage? Finally, each story about the president's personal life has had its unique characteristics, and we will address specific aspects of the Troopergate and Paula Jones allegations to determine whether there were certain factors inherent in each story that affected the media's coverage.

In Chapter Four, we address the lessons that ought to be learned from the coverage of Mr. Clinton's personal life. Clearly, media organizations need to approach such stories with deliberate and nuanced care. Difficult considerations of relevance are inherent in stories related to the personal lives of presidents and other public officials, and journalists' doubts about them are a legitimate part of the editorial evaluation process. Yet readers and viewers are not well served if *all* allegations about an officeholder's personal life are simply tossed into a basket marked "sex stories" and discarded. Some such stories are rightly ignored by the press, but others deserve public exposure. Developing standards for making these distinctions is critical to increasing the sophistication of press coverage in this vexing area of politics.

- TWO -

DIFFERENCES IN THE COVERAGE: WHITEWATER VS. TROOPERGATE/PAULA JONES

During the ten-month period we examined, the national press focused far more of its energies on Whitewater than on the sexual allegations made against President Clinton by both the Arkansas troopers and Paula Jones. The major media ran over six times as many TV and print stories on Whitewater and related events as on the president's alleged personal scandals. Treatment of the stories has also been different, as Whitewater stories of even modest importance were much more likely to reach the front page than those concerning the sex allegations.

In addition to the quantitative gap in the coverage of Whitewater and the sex stories, individual reporters and news organizations approached the two scandals in contradictory ways. As discussed below, much of this disparity can be explained by (1) the differing natures of Whitewater and the personal scandal stories; and (2) press judgments on the news value of Whitewater and the sex scandals. News organizations clearly demanded a higher standard of proof before publishing stories about Clinton's personal life than about new developments in the Whitewater story. The media also went much further to question the motives of the troopers and Paula Jones than the president's Whitewater accusers.

Little Coverage, With Exceptions

While most news organizations chose not to invest great resources in covering the Troopergate and Paula Jones stories, there were a couple of exceptions. On Troopergate, the *Los Angeles Times* devoted the most time among the major media. Reporter Bill Rempel worked on the story for four months and was later joined by another reporter, Douglas Frantz. On the Paula Jones matter, only the *Washington Post* initiated a serious investigation into the allegations that Ms. Jones made at her February 11 news conference.

Most media organizations devoted little effort to Troopergate even during the initial splash of attention generated by the publication of the *American Spectator* and *Los Angeles Times* stories. On the broadcast side, CNN was the most active, since it was given access to the troopers at the time of the release of the *American Spectator* piece. The troopers' attorney, well-known Clinton adversary Cliff Jackson, was concerned that the *Los Angeles Times* was not going to run the story. In the absence of the *Times*, he wanted another less ideological outlet for the troopers' tales than the *Spectator*.

CNN televised a fairly lengthy interview session with the troopers on Sunday, December 19, despite not having done much independent investigation of the troopers' claims. *Washington Post* media writer Howard Kurtz argued, "I think there was a real rush on the part of some organizations, once the story broke, to simply do quickie interviews and throw these guys on the air without having done some of the basic reporting. CNN, for example, had them on very quickly." (However, CNN sources claim the network had had some contacts with the troopers months earlier.)

CBS News had correspondent Scott Pelley interview the troopers for ten hours. But the network was uneasy about their charges and decided not to air anything from Pelley's long session. Other than CNN, ABC gave the most coverage to the Troopergate controversy. Yet even ABC did not have a reporter or producer working on the story after December 24. And despite its initial rush to air the story, CNN did little follow-up in the days after its initial trooper segment.

On the print side, all of the major outlets sent one or more journalists to Arkansas to cover the story, at least briefly. However, the only new information that resulted from the follow-up reports was a December 24 story by Michael Wines of the *New York Times*. He disclosed that the two on-the-record troopers, Roger Perry and Larry Patterson, had been involved in a fraudulent $100,000 insurance claim from a 1990 auto accident. For the most part, reporters sent to Little Rock to follow up on the story were home for Christmas. Moreover, no mainstream news organization admitted making a serious investigative attempt to examine the troopers' allegations more closely in the months following their public debut. (See Sidebar C, on pp. 79-84, for a case in point.)

In the Paula Jones case, only the *Washington Post* decided to look independently into her claims. The *Post*'s Michael Isikoff worked on the Jones story for several months. Later, the *Post* assigned reporters Sharon LaFraniere and Charles Shepard to do additional reporting. To our knowledge, no other major media outlets devoted resources to the Jones case prior to the period immediately preceding the filing of her lawsuit on May 6. After the lawsuit was filed, most large news organizations did send at least one reporter to Arkansas to cover Jones's allegations. But these excursions primarily focused on the history and character of Paula Jones, and little new reporting about the alleged incident came out of them.

The lack of resources expended on the Jones story may be even more notable than in the case of Troopergate, which had already been thoroughly reported by the *Los Angeles Times*. In that instance, editors and producers could somewhat reasonably argue that an effort to confirm what the *Times* had previously reported was a waste of time and money (although similar redundancies, especially on television, are common). This was clearly not the case with the Paula Jones matter, especially after her lightly reported news conference.

The minimal effort made by the press on the Troopergate and Paula Jones stories is in sharp contrast to the enormous investment of time and money spent covering Whitewater. All of the major news organizations have sent at least three or four reporters to Arkansas to develop leads on Whitewater. Most reporters working on the Whitewater story have been to Little Rock numerous times, and a few virtually lived there for months at a time during 1993 and 1994. "If I never go back to Little Rock, it will be fine with me," said one print reporter, reflecting the views of many of his investigative colleagues. Moreover, coverage of the Arkansas aspects of Whitewater represents only a small part of the enterprise, since dozens more reporters covered the Washington end of Whitewater news.

Stories Printed and Aired

Not surprisingly, the token effort to cover Troopergate and Paula Jones was reflected in the relative number of stories on the two sets of sexual allegations. Most newspapers carried the troopers' allegations on December 21, with the exception of the *Wall Street Journal,* which ignored the story in its news pages. In the following days, most major papers gave significant coverage to questions of the troopers' credibility, and many ran various subsidiary pieces on topics such as the Clinton administration's efforts to spin the story and the now-traditional follow-up on how their counterparts at other media outlets were covering the controversy.

Less than half (41 percent) of the stories run by the major newspapers dealt primarily or in much detail with the troopers' charges. (See Chart 1 on p. 120.) Those same papers ran very few Troopergate-related pieces after the start of 1994, and the general subject was raised again only with the advent of Paula Jones's tale and lawsuit. (See Graphs 1-2, pp. 112-113.) The *New York Times* was the most hesitant to publish the Clinton personal scandal stories, and the *Washington Times* the most eager. (See Sidebar D, pp. 85-90.)

The troopers' allegations were detailed in four *Newsweek* and seven *Time* articles, most of which were full-length features.

By contrast, *U.S. News & World Report* only broached the allegations in passing in one January 10 article. *U.S. News* reporter Greg Ferguson, when asked whether his magazine had ignored Troopergate, replied, "Yeah, they tried pretty hard to." *U. S. News* editor Lee Rainie defended his magazine's decision by pointing out that, "Our mission always is to give our readers something they can't get elsewhere... . We talked to the troopers and it was clear they told their stories very fully to the *Spectator* and the *L. A. Times* and... it's not like vast numbers of our readers didn't already know about [the charges]." Still, it is unusual for *U. S. News* not even to note the existence of a major story contemporaneously, if only with a short piece in the magazine's opening pages.

On the broadcast side, ABC aired the most stories (four) mentioning on the troopers' charges. ABC's Mike von Fremd, who did the initial, lengthy Troopergate report for his network, admitted that "when you have a story like this, the news division executives look at it very, very, very carefully." Even though ABC's interviews with the troopers were done on Saturday, December 18, the network held the story until Monday to double-check the troopers' employment records in the appropriate state offices, as well as to allow network brass and lawyers enough time to think it over. But in the end, said von Fremd, "We still felt an obligation [to air it] since [the charges] were being made for attribution by people with a responsible job."

NBC aired only one full-length story on the allegations, with borrowed CNN tape of the troopers. NBC correspondent Jim Miklaszewski said he spent hours on the telephone on Monday, December 20, trying to line up interviews with troopers Perry and Patterson, but "they had decided they weren't going to do anymore. One reason given was that one of the troopers had fallen ill. Whatever the excuse, they went underground, as is wont to happen."

In addition to not using Scott Pelley's interviews with the troopers, CBS did not air a single piece focusing exclusively on Troopergate and only briefly mentioned the allegations on December 22. As a group, the networks had essentially completed their sketchy coverage of Troopergate by Christmas Eve.

The number of stories on the Paula Jones case was similarly limited, at least until the lawsuit. Most of the major papers ran only brief stories the day after her February press conference. The exception was the *Washington Post*, which printed nothing at the time. In the run-up to the filing of the lawsuit and afterward, the *New York Times*, *Washington Post*, and *Los Angeles Times* combined to run a total of seventy-eight update stories related to the Jones matter. Among the news magazines, only *U.S. News* mentioned Jones's charges prior to the lawsuit. However, the three newsweeklies ran a total of thirty-four stories during and after the lawsuit's filing. (See Graph 3, p. 114.) Twenty-one of the thirty-five Jones stories were full-length pieces.

Among the "big three" networks, ABC once again devoted the most coverage to these personal allegations against the president. ABC's "World News Tonight" was the only evening news program that mentioned Ms. Jones's February press conference. Overall, eleven stories on ABC detailed her charges against Mr. Clinton, compared to four stories on CBS and only one on NBC.

The limited focus on the two sets of personal allegations against the president contrasts sharply with the bright media spotlight shone on Whitewater. Our study indentified 1,290 stories that focused on Whitewater-related news, compared to only 256 on all aspects of the allegations by Paula Jones and the Arkansas troopers.

Every major newspaper published more than five times the number of stories on Whitewater as on Troopergate/Paula Jones. (See Graph 5, p. 116.) During only two months (December and May) did the number of personal scandal stories outnumber the Whitewater articles. (See Graph 6, p. 117.) The networks were even more one-sided, with a total of eight Whitewater stories aired for each one about Troopergate and Paula Jones combined — 277 vs. 34 respectively. (See Graph 7, p. 118.)

In the overall news agenda, the two personal scandals were about equal in visibility to relatively minor aspects of the Whitewater story. (See Charts 2 and 3, p. 121.) For example, the networks mentioned possible document shredding at the Rose Law Firm about as often as they did the troopers' allegations. Likewise, the *New York Times, Washington Post,* and *Los Angeles Times* combined to run more stories on Hillary Rodham Clinton's commodities trading than they did on the specifics of Paula Jones's sexual harassment complaint.

Standards of Proof

Beyond this disparity in the number of stories, there were also differences in how news organizations handled the two scandals. For example, the standards of proof required for the respective accusations varied greatly. In both the Troopergate and Paula Jones cases, the seminal article in the major media was withheld from publication for a substantial period. (See Sidebars A and B for a discussion of the publication delays in the *Los Angeles Times* story on the trooper allegations, as well as the *Washington Post* story on Paula Jones's accusations.)

Los Angeles Times reporters Rempel and Frantz had completed their reporting on Troopergate by the middle of December 1993. All of the *Times* editors, with the exception of Editor-in-Chief Shelby Coffey, were prepared to run the story. In the following week two notable decisions were made. First, Coffey sent the reporters to Washington to show the story to Jack Nelson, the *Times* Washington Bureau Chief. Despite rumors at the time, Nelson was not opposed to running the story and did not threaten to resign over it. But he did suggest the *Times* should administer lie detector tests to the troopers, who had agreed to submit to them.

Due to logistical problems, the tests were never performed. But the request was unusual since such tests are of dubious validity, and a paper normally trusts its reporters to judge the veracity of sources and to corroborate their stories in other ways.

Moreover, the *Times* did not seek to perform lie detector tests on witnesses such as Whitewater's David Hale, who was under indictment on felony fraud charges at the time he was interviewed by the same two reporters.

A second debatable decision was also made while Rempel and Frantz were in Washington. Understandably, the paper wanted to get a response from the White House before running the story. Therefore, on Thursday, December 16, the reporters submitted their questions to the White House. Less understandably, Coffey decided that the paper would not give the White House a deadline for their response. This only encouraged Clinton aides to stall. (See Sidebar A.) It is highly likely that with a Whitewater-related story, the *Times* (or any other paper) simply would have said to the White House, "Here's what we've got, we'll let you respond if you want but we're going to run it shortly regardless."

The *Washington Post's* handling of the Paula Jones story points to other ways in which the burden of proof varied depending on the type of story. First, when the *Post* decided not to print Jones's accusations the day after her news conference, Executive Editor Leonard Downie was quoted in the *Post* as saying, "When allegations are made by people in public, if they are not law enforcement officials, we like to check into them ourselves before printing them." This is a defensible policy that ultimately produced responsible and thorough coverage.

Yet this policy did not seem to apply to all stories. Take, for example, the *Post's* December 19 front-page piece on the Clintons' claimed Whitewater losses ["Clintons' Arkansas Land Venture Losses Disputed"]. Reporters Howard Schnieder and Charles R. Babcock quoted Chris Wade, a real estate agent who had managed the Whitewater Development Corporation in the 1980's, as saying, "I don't see where they would have lost money." The reporters had checked Wade's background enough to discover that he had been criticized by banking regulators about his past land deals. Nonetheless, they used Wade, a fairly unknown source and certainly not a law enforcement official, to claim without documentation that the President of the United States was lying about losing money on Whitewater. By March, records were released demonstrating that the *Post*'s source was far off the mark. The Clintons had lost $47,000, less than their original claim of $69,000, but still a substantial amount.

Most notable about the *Post's* treatment of the Jones story was the fact that the story was held by the editors for several months, even though most of the material that eventually appeared had been collected within the first few weeks after her February press conference. The *Post* took the unusual step of assigning two additional reporters to retrace the work that had been done by Michael Isikoff, the original reporter investigating the charges. (See Sidebar B.) No such steps were taken on any of the major Whitewater stories run by the paper.

Concerning the decision to hold the Jones story for several months, the *Post* was criticized by conservatives such as Reed Irvine of the media-watchdog group Accuracy in Media. They charged that the paper was trying to protect the president by not publishing damaging information. In fact, opponents of the president might well have praised the *Post* for being the only major news organization to take Jones's allegations seriously. It is true, however, that some editors at the *Post* were reluctant to print the story because of doubts about the story's validity and its relevance to the Clinton presidency. (See Sidebar B.)

The *Post's* internal debate and its extensive rechecking of the facts added many weeks to the story's journey through the newspaper's editorial labyrinth. And in the end, the decision to publish was partly determined by external events. The paper's top editors did not want to print the Jones material on its own, but rather in the context of another story. Mr. Clinton's hiring of high-profile attorney Robert Bennett to defend him against Jones's charges provided this opportunity. The contrast with the *Post's* Whitewater coverage is clear: At no time was an external catalyst needed to prompt the *Post's* publication of a major Whitewater story.

Treatment of Sources

None of the prominent accusers in Whitewater and Mr. Clinton's personal affairs is a nominee for sainthood. Troopers Perry and Patterson were implicated in the 1990 insurance scheme mentioned earlier. Paula Jones, according to one of her sisters, is looking for money in her suit against the president. James McDougal ran an S&L into the ground at a cost to taxpayers of $60 million, and he is currently under investigation for misusing depositor funds at Madison Guaranty. David Hale has already pled guilty to a felony fraud charge for misusing Small Business Administration loans. But saints are rarely found at the scene of a scandal. The key question for reporters and editors has been how to account for the accusers' credibility problems.

In the case of the troopers, their believability was diminished in the eyes of many journalists after the *New York Times* reported that they had falsified a $100,000 claim against an insurance company. The *Times'* Michael Wines, who authored the story, suggested that his revelations "ended the [Troopergate] story right there to a large extent." Indeed, most major media outlets ran nothing more on Troopergate after his December 24 story.

Troopergate could easily have unfolded differently. After the Wines story was published, *Los Angeles Times* reporters Rempel and Frantz were criticized for not having uncovered the same information during their original investigation. But the reporters had actually included the insurance scam in a 1,500-word sidebar about the troopers' history. Editors at the *Times* decided that they would not run the sidebar, but rather would incorporate the information into the main story. Unfortunately for the *Times*, at some point in the last-minute editing process the information about the insurance scandal was dropped.

Had the insurance story been a part of the original *Los Angeles Times* article, the life span of Troopergate coverage might have been extended. If the troopers' credibility problems had been acknowledged up front, then that aspect of the story might not have seemed so damning. As it was, however, the insurance fraud case offered jittery journalists an excuse to drop Troopergate.

How does this compare with the handling of credibility questions about some of those making serious allegations in the Whitewater case? David Hale, a former judge in Arkansas, has levied perhaps the most serious Whitewater allegation against the president. Hale claims that as governor, Mr. Clinton urged him to make a $300,000 SBA-sponsored loan to Susan McDougal. With $120,000 of the loan eventually going to Whitewater, Hale asserts that Mr. Clinton asked for the loan to help offset Whitewater's financial troubles. At the time Hale originally made these charges, however, he was under indictment on felony fraud charges relating to the improper use of SBA-backed loans. (He subsequently pled guilty to a single felony charge in exchange for offering information to then-special counsel Robert Fiske.)

Clearly, Hale had a powerful incentive to concoct a false story, since it could help him avoid prison. Every lengthy story written or aired by the major media about Hale's allegations have put the charges in the proper context of a felon's background and possible motivations. Yet Hale's past deeds and current motives have not completely sullied him as a witness in the eyes of most news organizations. Thus, questions about Hale's credibility have not distracted from the coverage of his claims. As one reporter familiar with Whitewater put it, "You don't usually get saints to implicate sinners. They just don't hang out together." It is apparent, however, that sinners make credible enough witnesses for a traditional financial scandal, but not for stories of a more distasteful personal nature.

In the Paula Jones case, the most significant factors in diminishing her credibility were the facts that she was sponsored by Clinton antagonist Cliff Jackson and originally made her allegations at a conservative conference. Understandable skepticism greeted her charges, given the partisan nature of both her principal handler and the setting for her news conference. "Here was a story coming out of a conservative forum with an ax to grind, and that put [journalists] on edge," observed Fred Barnes of the *New Republic*.

In the case of Whitewater, however, hard-core opponents of the president have also played a significant role in driving the story. Cliff Jackson — of Troopergate and Paula Jones fame — was involved, as was Arkansas Republican politician Sheffield Nelson. Conservative activists Floyd Brown and David Bossie, who have devoted themselves to discrediting the Clintons, have also provided much information to reporters. The efforts of Brown and Bossie were documented in an April 19 article by *Washington Post* media writer Howard Kurtz. They facilitated reporters' access to Clinton accuser David Hale. They showed journalists a 1988 letter in which Hillary Clinton requested from James McDougal the power of attorney over the Whitewater Development Corporation. They even gave reporters copies of a recorded conversation in which McDougal told Clinton's 1990 Republican gubernatorial opponent Nelson that he could refute the Clintons' claimed Whitewater losses.

Brown told Kurtz that reporters from CBS and ABC had come to see his information. He also claimed that he had "worked directly with NBC News, helping them every step of the way...." NBC investigative reporter Ira Silverman responded, "You don't find swans in the sewer." All of the reporters who have received records from these individuals insist that they have always independently verified what they have gotten. Nonetheless, the fact that the original information or guidance on Whitewater comes from staunch foes of Clinton has not deterred reporters from pursuing such stories.

Finally, after the Paula Jones lawsuit was filed, numerous media outlets made a concerted effort to highlight less flattering personal qualities about her in a way that was rarely done with controversial figures in Whitewater. For example, *U.S. News & World Report*, *Newsweek* and the *Washington Post* all ran profiles of Jones that were filled with subjective and sometimes vicious appraisals of her character. The *U.S. News* piece, for example, declared that, "Friends and relatives now publicly call her a flirt, a ditz, a jezebel... and the national media portray her as a white trash bimbo."

On the whole, Jones and the troopers reaped the media whirlwind, as Graph 8 shows. (See p. 119.) Jones's broadcast news coverage was 67 percent negative and only 33 percent positive, with Troopers Perry and Patterson faring even worse (77 percent negative, 23 percent positive). For all of his mounting political problems, President Clinton — the object of Jones's and the troopers' allegations — received much kinder overall treatment from network news. From November 1, 1993 to August 15, 1994, almost half (49 percent) of all evaluations of Mr. Clinton's behavior in scandal-related news stories supported the president. And one of the key players in the Whitewater scandal, James McDougal, survived his network coverage in better shape than Jones, Perry, and Patterson. McDougal's positive coverage was 38 percent of the total, while 62 percent was negative.

When dealing with sources in the Whitewater case, such as Hale or McDougal, journalists were generally careful to provide important background information about the accusers. Yet in most cases, news organizations did not run profiles that called their essential credibility into question, much less print or air highly negative personal characterizations. None of the major outlets offered a specific profile of Hale, and only the *Washington Post* and NBC profiled McDougal. This was despite the fact that one national reporter familiar with the subject described McDougal, a key figure at the center of the Whitewater story, as a "certifiable lunatic." Once again, news organizations displayed standards for Whitewater that were somewhat different from those in evidence during Troopergate or the Paula Jones affair.

* * * * * * * * * * * *

In summary, a detailed examination of the stories generated by the alleged Clinton scandals reveals that (1) Whitewater was heavily covered while the sexual allegations were barely touched by most media outlets; (2) the standards of proof news organizations required for airing Whitewater-related charges were lower than those they demanded for the troopers' and Ms. Jones's accusations; and (3) Whitewater sources often received more respectful treatment than the principal accusers of the other scandals. The question that remains is why these differences occurred.

- THREE -

WHY JOURNALISTS WERE RELUCTANT TO COVER THE PERSONAL SCANDALS

As the previous discussion has made clear, the press was reluctant to report and follow up on the Troopergate and Paula Jones stories. But why was this the case? Among the numerous explanations explored below, perhaps most telling is the mainstream media's general unease about dealing with sexual issues — even in the era of tabloid journalism — particularly when they involve the President of the United States.

Other factors include the media's inability to see the more important allegations that were hidden behind a sexual facade. Also present were certain distractions in both stories that offered journalists easy justifications for not covering them. And while Troopergate featured legs aplenty, it lacked a special kind of journalistic "legs." In the other personal scandal, a class consciousness and social elitism affected the presentation of Paula Jones's allegations.

Squeamish on Sex: Values of the Media

Many journalists were reluctant to dwell on these allegations because of their own aversion to using sexual behavior as a measure of character. In general, members of the national media hold relatively permissive or "liberal" attitudes with regard to sexual behavior. In their book *The Media Elite*, Robert Lichter, Stanley Rothman and Linda Lichter found that only a minority of leading journalists were willing to condemn adultery. As part of a larger survey, they asked 240 randomly selected journalists from ten national news organizations to agree or disagree with the following statement: "It is wrong for a married person to have sexual relations with someone other than his or her spouse." Only 47 percent responded that adultery was wrong, and only 15 percent "agreed strongly" that extramarital affairs were wrong. Among a dozen elite groups whom these researchers polled, only the Hollywood creative community proved as tolerant on this issue as the media elite. (Among the general public, surveys consistently find that at least 80 percent regard adultery as wrong.)

While journalism is not an ideological monolith on sex (or anything else), the comments of ABC's Jim Wooten seem fairly representative of the predominant view among the mainstream press:

> Reagan used to tell these off-color, locker-room stories about his Hollywood swordsmanship to people that he trusted, including a couple of reporters I know, mentioning names of famous Hollywood female stars that he had bedded. And he was divorced, and Nancy was pregnant when they got married. And nobody cared... And this fellow, Clinton... I don't have any interest in who he was sleeping with then or who he's screwing now. It doesn't make any difference to me.

Unquestionably, many Americans agree wholly or partly with Wooten. Opinion surveys have often found that the public says it cares more about a president's official performance than his personal life. But these polls may well understate the electorate's concerns about presidential character, and President Clinton's unpopularity can be traced in some measure to his weakness on this score. As Gloria Borger, an Assistant Managing Editor for *U.S. News & World Report*, notes:

> What matters is that in some form, people are talking about [the Clintons'] marriage, and while voters say character doesn't matter, in the end [President] Clinton's polls have suffered because of the character issue. In

some way, while the public says "we think it's irrelevant," they [actually] believe it *is* relevant.

Moreover, there is a significant minority of Americans who
care deeply about personal character issues. These include Chris-
tian conservatives and others who hold firm religious or moral
beliefs about infidelity, and who consider character to be of
paramount importance in a leader. Brit Hume, ABC's senior
White House correspondent and a conservative, regrets the failure of his colleagues to consider the views of what he calls the
"other America." He also sees a contradiction in journalists'
own approach to the subject:

> You hear an almost mantra-like refrain that [the charac-
> ter issue] isn't really what people care about. What
> people really care about is health care. It is striking that
> journalists say nobody cares about [sexual fidelity], and
> then the news organizations that *do* publish stories about
> it will be accused of trying to boost their circulation or
> ratings. I think journalists actually believe people care
> like mad about sex. It's just that sex is not what they
> want to be specializing in.

Clearly, reporters and editors need to make judgments about
the news value of particular stories. But when those judgments
are based primarily on their own personal values, the concerns of
large segments of their audience are discounted. Assuming
sufficient proof exists to print or air a charge, journalists need to
take a broad view of their readership or viewership, always
remembering that the residents of the average newsroom are
highly unrepresentative of the public in many ways, and especially in the realm of social values and political ideology.

Journalists' Self-Esteem

Another factor that discourages reporters from seeking out
stories involving the tawdry is their view of themselves as professionals. Most national journalists tried to avoid Troopergate
and Paula Jones because they deemed such lowbrow scandals to

be unworthy of their attention. Says ABC's Hume of most of his colleagues in the national press corps:

> They think it's unseemly to cover this sort of stuff...
> They have come to Washington to cover the serious
> issues of the day, and this is back-stairs gossip. Even if
> it's true, its relevance is at least questionable, and some-
> thing they're not in the business to do and become
> known for doing.

At an early stage in the *Los Angeles Times's* Troopergate investigation, some editors are frank to admit they searched for a way out. The first two *Times* editors to deal with the subject, Roger Smith and Mike Miller, both had negative visceral reac- tions. As Smith remembered it, "In some ways we were all looking for relief, for some way we could avoid this. At one point, Mike Miller said, 'This is a sex story and I really don't like it.'" Similarly there was initial reluctance at the *Washington Post* to reopen the book on Bill Clinton's personal life. Reporter Sharon LaFraniere, who took up not only the Paula Jones story but also other alleged instances of Clinton's infidelity, recalled being "uncomfortable. It's not a lot of fun to ask people, 'Did you sleep with somebody and how did that come about?'"

The perceived stigma attached to covering distasteful sexual allegations affects not only individual reporters but also news organizations. In the case of Troopergate, the media's obvious desire to drop the story in December 1993 may have helped fuel the frenzied attention given to Whitewater in the weeks that followed. The *Washington Post's* media writer, Howard Kurtz, is one of those who subscribes to this theory, saying:

> There is absolutely a connection there. For journalists
> who felt uncomfortable or dirty pursuing these allega-
> tions of infidelity, Whitewater was the perfect scandal.
> High-minded. Financial. Dry. I don't have any doubt
> that a lot of news organizations redoubled their efforts
> on Whitewater to show that they were not soft on Bill

Clinton, even though they weren't going to dive into the muck of Troopergate.

Similarly and more generally, it may be that the media's extremely tough critique of the Clinton administration's policies — documented by the Center for Media and Public Affairs' research — has been partly a substitute for, or a channelling of, journalists' disapproval of Clinton's private activities. (Even if they chose not to put it into print or onto the airwaves, most reporters were well versed in the details of allegations about Mr. Clinton's sexual behavior.)

Another motive for deemphasizing Mr. Clinton's personal behavior was journalists' revulsion at the tabloid and ideological sources pushing the stories to the fore. Those who report for prestigious national publications are perched in elite positions at the top of journalism's hierarchy. At the bottom of the journalistic order (at least in the view of those at the top) are those who work for tabloids or overtly ideological publications. The hierarchy breaks down, to the distress of the elite, whenever the mainstream press is forced to follow the lead of tabloids, as with the *Star*-generated Gennifer Flowers story in early 1992. Such painful memories may have affected the willingness to give ample attention to Troopergate. As the *New Republic's* Fred Barnes argued: "There's an antipathy to this type of story [Troopergate] partly because people in the mainstream press feel the new media [are] breathing down their neck."

The central role played by the conservative *American Spectator* in bringing Troopergate to light certainly had a dampening effect on mainstream media, despite the fact that the *Los Angeles Times* subsequently published many of the same allegations. David Brock, the author of the Spectator piece, was also highly controversial and unpopular with the press corps, in part because his book, *The Real Anita Hill,* attempted to debunk Hill's charges against Supreme Court nominee Clarence Thomas. The *Post's* Howard Kurtz believes that the "Brock factor" was a significant one: "While Brock may have brought some of it on himself, it may have been easier [for reporters] to demonize David Brock as a sort of tabloid-style reporter for the right wing than to seriously grapple with whether what he reported was true." Brit Hume argues that, beyond journalistic elitism, political bias also played a role:

> The treatment of David Brock by his fellow journalists is one of the more remarkable stories in recent journalistic history. It was so extreme. *Newsweek* referred to him as a journalist with the word journalist in quotes. Michael Kinsley refused to appear on the air with him on "Crossfire," of all programs. Whatever anyone might think of David Brock, it is clear that he is a journalist. He is manifestly a journalist. What's more, by any objective standard, his reporting... was pretty careful.... It bespeaks of unmistakable bias. One can hardly imagine the same treatment being accorded to some journalist on the left.

Peer Review and Public Reaction

Like all professionals, reporters seek approval from, and fear the condemnation of, their peers. And given a choice, they much prefer to be loved rather than hated by the public. Both peers and public appear to regard sex stories as déclassé. This in turn has produced much ambivalence in the press corps about publishing or airing a major story involving the president's personal life, especially if one leads the pack. As a reporter for one of the weekly news magazines said, "I don't really want to be the first to do one of these stories. I don't think [the magazine] wants to be the first to do one of these stories."

Such reluctance is unusual in a fiercely aggressive and highly competitive group of journalists. A "normal" scandal such as Whitewater finds the media enveloped in a frenzied struggle to be the first to report any major development. *In the case of Troopergate and the Paula Jones story, the mainstream media were locked in a race to be second.* This race for the silver medal resulted not just from the media's general discomfort with the subject matter, but also from concerns about how the story would be received by peers and the public.

When a story such as Troopergate is published, a great deal of Monday-morning quarterbacking takes place among journalists on talk shows and other venues about the propriety of such reporting. Invariably, many of those who broach the topic do so because they find such stories unseemly. These critics typically attack the early reporting of their colleagues. For example, *New York Times* columnist Anthony Lewis, writing on Christmas Eve in the aftermath of the original Troopergate stories, targeted those who scooped the field: "In the last week the American press has faced — and most of it flunked — a test of its resistance to the cheap and scurrilous."

It's the President, Stupid

One factor that clearly distinguishes Troopergate and the Paula Jones story from other recent allegations of sex scandals (such as those involving Clarence Thomas and Bob Packwood) is the fact that the target of the allegations is the President of the United States. With journalists uneasy about sex stories to begin with, the fact that the stories involve the president seems to magnify their aversion to covering them. This response is atypical, since most journalists believe that the occupant of the nation's highest office ought to be subject to the greatest scrutiny of all.

The explanation for this apparent contradiction is simple: Despite their inherently adversarial position relative to all government officials, and despite their general unhappiness with President Clinton and his White House (See Sidebar E, pp. 91-96.), few in the mainstream media would take comfort from diminishing the office of the presidency without a reason of constitutional proportions.

This perspective alters the standards that journalists use for personal scandal stories. In discussing CBS's decision not to air its interviews with the troopers, for example, correspondent Scott Pelley offered a revealing statement: "It just seemed a little bit tenuous, and you want to rise to a higher standard when dealing with the office of the Presidency of the United States." The higher standard of which Pelley speaks, however, seems only to apply to stories involving the president's personal life. Jack Nelson, the Washington Bureau Chief for the *Los Angeles Times*, pointed out that quite the opposite has been true in the coverage of Whitewater: "There have been a lot of Whitewater stories that have been very thinly sourced and much below the standard that we used to require for investigative reporting."

The difference in standards results in part from the potential effects of the two kinds of stories. A traditional scandal, short of one with impeachable offenses found in a mega-frenzy such as Watergate, certainly damages an individual president's credibility. Nonetheless, a skillful politician can emerge with political stature intact. Coverage of a president's personal scandals, however, can produce a type of embarrassment that permanently damages the moral authority necessary for governance.

This fact--and the media's reluctance to cover such matters-- was certainly recognized by the White House, which launched a major damage control operation on Troopergate. One of President Clinton's top aides and old Arkansas friends, Bruce Lindsey, was caught on tape by ABC News giving instructions to R. L. "Buddy" Young, a former Arkansas trooper who remained loyal to Mr. Clinton as Troopergate unfolded. (After Mr. Clinton's election, non-college graduate Young was appointed to a $92,000-a-year job at the Federal Emergency Management Agency.) Aired on December 20, 1993 during "World News Tonight," the ABC segment recorded a telephone call that came in from Lindsey to Young, while ABC was in the process of doing an interview with Young. Foolishly, Young put his phone on speaker and did not tell the camera crew to stop rolling tape. As a result, Lindsey's directive that he talk to the networks about Troopergate became part of the story.

ABC's Mike von Fremd saw up close yet another part of the White House's damage control, under the command of former Clinton gubernatorial aide Betsey Wright (who performed a similar role for Mr. Clinton's 1992 presidential campaign). Just as Troopergate was "going public" in late December 1993, Ms. Wright journeyed from Washington to Arkansas to visit Trooper Danny Ferguson, one of the key sources for both the *Spectator* and the *Los Angeles Times*. Wright not only "visited" with Ferguson, she arranged to see his wife, an employee of current Democratic Governor Jim Guy Tucker. The meeting with Mrs. Ferguson was held at the governor's mansion in the presence of Governor Tucker, according to von Fremd. Shortly thereafter, Trooper Ferguson issued an ambiguous "affidavit" through his lawyer, appearing to backtrack on his charges that President Clinton had made a job-for-silence offer to him in September 1993.

Actually, the attorney's statement said only that no *specific* quid pro quo was proposed. As Ferguson later made clear to the *Los Angeles Times*, the trooper believed the job offer was implicit in Mr. Clinton's words. But some news organizations, already uncomfortable with Troopergate, used Ferguson's supposed recantation to step away from the controversy — exactly Wright's intent. Meanwhile, von Fremd was repeatedly trying to contact the Fergusons, but "there was nobody home. I found out that they both had gone on vacation for three critical weeks, just after [Betsey Wright] left. I could never reach either one of them. It seemed to me to be more than a coincidence... . Talk about damage control! That's pretty clever."

Sex vs. Official Misconduct: Have the Media Missed the Most Important Aspects of Clinton's Personal Scandals?

TROOPERGATE: INFIDELITY OR IMPROPRIETY?

The immediate response of many journalists to the troopers' allegations was that Bill Clinton's messy personal life while governor of Arkansas had no relevance to his presidency. R. W. Apple, Jr., the Washington Bureau Chief of the *New York Times*, insisted at the time, "I am not interested in Bill Clinton's sex life as governor of Arkansas. I'm certain there are a lot of readers who are interested in that, and there are lots of publications they can turn to to slake that thirst." [As quoted in the *Washington Post* on December 22, 1993.]

Similarly, Scott Pelley of CBS remembered that after his interviews with the troopers, "We just felt, not to sound pompous in any way, but it didn't rise to the level of something that we wanted to put on the 'Evening News.'" And Eleanor Clift of *Newsweek* reflected the views of many in her profession when she said, "I think it's [the Clintons'] private life. If he's had affairs, if they've resolved it between themselves, what business is it of ours?" As noted earlier, these kinds of reactions resulted in news organizations such as the *Wall Street Journal, U.S. News & World Report*, and CBS essentially ignoring the story.

Yet this perspective begs two distinct questions about the media's handling of Troopergate. First, to what extent is the personal life of the president actually "no business of ours," or do some very private matters still have public consequences? Second, even if we assume that the president's personal life is truly irrelevant, was that in fact the most important aspect of the Troopergate story?

To a large extent, the lurid details of Mr. Clinton's alleged promiscuity were a backdrop in the Troopergate story to more important and traditional forms of political misconduct: the misuse of state employees as governor, and offers (however vague) of federal jobs in exchange for the troopers' silence. Not all journalists missed this crucial dimension of the story. In late December 1993, *Washington Post* Managing Editor Leonard Downie, Jr. explained in his newspaper the *Post's* decision to publish information about Troopergate this way:

> Extramarital affairs is not the subject of our reporting. The subject of our reporting is whether or not Bill

Clinton, as governor and now as president, has in any way used resources and power in any connection with his private life that would be improper.

The original stories alleged that Mr. Clinton used the state troopers to help facilitate his assignations, as well as to perform other personal work. Regardless of the sexual context, such allegations, if true, would represent a corrupt use of power (albeit before Mr. Clinton was president). Unquestionably, the press would have been drawn like a magnet to a case of such traditional impropriety if the backdrop had not been sex.

Perhaps most significantly, the original *Los Angeles Times* investigative story alleged that Bill Clinton *as president* had contacted at least one of the troopers, Danny Ferguson, and offered him a federal position in order to keep silent on Mr. Clinton's past. In a CNN interview shortly after publication, Douglas Frantz, one of the *Los Angeles Times*'s story's authors, stressed this very point, stating that, "It's not about sex... it's about the President of the United States making calls repeatedly to troopers at a time when he knew they were about to go forward with information that could be harmful to him."

Not only was this potentially another instance of the corrupt use of office, but it was also the one Troopergate allegation that pertained to Bill Clinton as president. For this reason, some reporters declared this one aspect of the story to be legitimate. Yet even it faded quickly from print and air because of a further development. Several days after Troopergate broke, Danny Ferguson, one of the previously off-the-record troopers, came forward to disavow his claim of a jobs-for-silence offer. Much of the media reported that he had issued an "affidavit" recanting his story. As noted earlier, however, Ferguson merely issued a statement through a lawyer that was *not* a sworn affidavit and that simply said Mr. Clinton had not *specifically* offered a federal position as a quid pro quo for silence. The original charge was still intact, but Ferguson's phantom affidavit seemed to dampen whatever enthusiasm the national press may have had for the federal jobs angle of Troopergate.

This is not the first time that the press has sprinted away from a Clinton sex story and left a vital, non-sexual aspect of the story unexamined. As ABC's Jim Wooten recalled about the Gennifer Flowers charges:

> The most important thing about that story was that he got her a job... ***not***, "was he good in bed" or "what are his dimensions".... The important thing was she said, and there was fairly clear backup for this, that he arranged for her to get a job in state government, and managed for her to keep it, even though she didn't have much interest in it or many skills appropriate to it.

PAULA JONES — WOMANIZING OR HARASSMENT?

Most of the mainstream media were as reluctant to report the most "legitimate" angle of the Paula Jones story — on-the-job sexual harassment of a low-level employee by a powerful boss — as they were Troopergate's jobs-for-silence component or the earlier employment of Gennifer Flowers. A few journalists, such as the *New Republic's* conservative commentator Fred Barnes, argued that Jones's potential case of harassment had more resonance than Troopergate because "the nature of the accusation was different. It was a trendier crime. It was sexual harassment rather than just womanizing."

Nonetheless, most of his colleagues did not much focus on this supposedly "trendy crime," classifying her claim as just another unseemly and irrelevant sex story, no more credible than the troopers' tales. Others, such as *Boston Globe* Editor Matthew Storin, remembered the press's treatment of Clarence Thomas and believed fairness dictated an equally serious look at this new charge of sexual harassment: "The guiding principle in my mind was that we must treat this in some manner of proportion to the way we treated the Anita Hill charges." [As quoted in the *Washington Post*, May 14, 1994.]

The press had come to know Anita Hill, and unquestionably they regarded Paula Jones as no Anita Hill. Elements of ideological suspicion and cultural condescension combined to produce coverage that could not have been more different in quality and quantity than that accorded the polished law professor in 1991. (This subject will be taken up again later.)

An Easy Exit Strategy

If the media's unease about covering the president's personal life made reporters apprehensive about Troopergate and Paula Jones, then certain elements of each story gave them the easy excuses they needed to ignore or downplay the allegations. Most of the justifications offered by the press were wrapped in the language of journalistic professionalism. Yet these highlighted standards of good journalism were selectively applied to produce an easy exit strategy for an unsettled press. Seven such factors are outlined below.

1. IT'S OLD NEWS

Perhaps the most consistent refrain coming from those who were reluctant to leap into the president's sex scandals was that Troopergate and (to a lesser extent) Paula Jones were "old news." For example, one editor defended his publication's minimal coverage of Troopergate by arguing, "The general notion that Bill and Hillary Clinton had a troubled marriage at times and that he might not have been a faithful husband was something that was out there and processed by the voters."

Newsweek's Eleanor Clift offered similar sentiments on Paula Jones's original news conference: "The initial reluctance [to cover it] came from a sense that in a way this was old news." Clift added that the Jones case did not really become a story until she filed a lawsuit against the president in May, an opinion with which many of her colleagues concurred. Others suggested that only the president's hiring of super-lawyer Robert Bennett made the allegations genuine news, since it demonstrated that the White House was taking the charges seriously.

Prior to the lawsuit, however, many journalists insisted that both Ms. Jones's and the troopers' allegations were about an old issue that was "resolved" with the Gennifer Flowers frenzy of January 1992, and the Clintons' subsequent appearance on "60 Minutes," where Bill Clinton acknowledged causing "pain" in his marriage. According to this popular interpretation, the new sex stories were irrelevant because voters had earlier digested the fact that Mr. Clinton had been unfaithful to his wife while governor of Arkansas, but elected him president anyway.

On closer inspection, this argument appears dubious. First, as discussed earlier, both the Troopergate and Jones stories made other allegations against the president apart from infidelity, including harassment, misuse of public personnel, and jobs-for-silence offers. Second, the original stories in the *Los Angeles Times* and the *American Spectator* alleged that the promiscuity had continued after the Gennifer Flowers incident, and even after the November 1992 election. While the overall relevance and factual accuracy of this information could be disputed, members of the media were manifestly incorrect to argue that such charges were not new.

2. THEY DID IT FOR MONEY

Another media justification for not paying heed to the troopers was the belief that they were supposedly telling their story for financial gain. Greg Ferguson of *U.S. News & World Report* said of the troopers, "They all sort of cut deals." In fact, none of the troopers has been able to turn his story into gold. Bill Rempel of the *Los Angeles Times*, the first reporter to speak with the troopers, said financial motivations played a fairly limited role for at least two of the accusing officers:

> I believe two of the troopers [Roger Perry and Larry Patterson] were not doing it for money ever.... Did they want to get some money? Yeah, but that wasn't why they were doing it. In the end they went public without [any money] and haven't received much of anything

since.... . Two of the [other troopers] thought they could get some money, and there was [once] the potential for big money. And when [these two] saw that wasn't going to happen, they wouldn't [agree to] have their names in the story.

However, mere *rumors* about a book deal for the troopers were featured prominently in the initial coverage, and this seemed to turn many journalists away from the story. What was rarely mentioned in follow-up articles was that the troopers had put themselves in a vulnerable situation, socially and professionally, in the small world of Little Rock. Rempel told the troopers from the outset that their lives would be torn apart in Arkansas and that other reporters were sure to rummage through their past. (See Sidebar A.)

In the end, the media chose to focus on the troopers' potential financial gain, which was never realized, while ignoring the stigma that might (and did) stain their lives in Arkansas. The former offered news organizations an additional reason to steer clear of Troopergate, while the latter might have encouraged more reflection on the serious charges that were made.

3. THE ACCUSERS WERE "DISCREDITED" AND "INCREDIBLE"

Among our interviewees who were closest to Troopergate, nearly all believed the troopers were substantially telling the truth, and most sensed this from the outset. Moreover, as NBC White House correspondent Jim Miklaszewski observed, most accepted and credited the troopers' unique vantage point:

Anybody who has ever covered a president or a governor knows that his security force becomes a second skin around him. If anybody has intimate knowledge of what a president or governor does in private, it would be these guys.... The very fact that these troopers spent as much time as they did in off hours with Governor Clinton lent some credibility to their stories.

Nonetheless, after it was reported in the *New York Times* that troopers Perry and Patterson had admitted to lying in a 1990 auto insurance scheme, the words "damaged credibility" seemed almost inextricably linked to their names in Troopergate stories. Some journalists questioned whether the 1990 incident *should* have discredited the troopers. Bill Rempel of the *Los Angeles Times* insisted that the stories about the troopers' involvement in the insurance scheme represented "a gross misunderstanding of the realities of the case" and suggested the troopers had not actually engaged in fraud. His editor, Roger Smith, strongly agreed:

> We looked into that carefully, and it wasn't insurance fraud at all. In fact, all it amounted to was that in order to get an insurance payment made [after an accident with a state car], one of them had to sue the insurance company of the other. It was the normal course of events in a case of this kind.

Even if the troopers were guilty of the fraud alleged in the *New York Times*, one past instance of dishonesty does not necessarily impeach their extensive and detailed testimony, much of which was corroborated by existing records and state documents. And once again, the press had a much lower threshold of credibility for some sources in the Whitewater scandal. The alleged wrongdoings of Roger Perry and Larry Patterson pale in comparison to the very serious charges levied against David Hale and James McDougal. Yet *New York Times* reporter Jeff Gerth could reasonably say of Hale, "We certainly knew that he wasn't a saint, but that doesn't automatically make him a liar." The same could be said of the troopers.

One further argument about the relative credibility of these scandal witnesses emerged from our interviews. The journalists and editors most closely involved in both scandal investigations — the very people whose instincts and experience are vital to their news organizations' judgments about the believability of sources — generally found the troopers, and to a lesser extent,

Paula Jones, credible about their basic allegations, while serious doubts were raised about the statements of Hale and McDougal.

Concerning the troopers, these comments by reporters were typical:

- ABC's Jim Wooten: "Yeah, I think they were telling the truth."

- The *New Republic's* Fred Barnes: "I believe the thrust of their stories. I haven't found the denials very convincing."

- The *Los Angeles Times's* Bill Rempel: "When we were done reporting, we didn't have any doubt that the stories we heard were true in substance."

As to Paula Jones, most journalists remain unsure about the veracity of her sexual harassment allegations, and about the specific details of her private session with then-Governor Clinton. Nonetheless, as Brit Hume of ABC observed, "The virtually unanimous view is that Bill Clinton and Paula Jones were in that [hotel] room... and that he came on to her. I think everybody accepts that."

By contrast, some of the reporters who interviewed Hale and McDougal seemed less impressed with their credibility:

- Wooten on Hale: "I think his credibility is fragile."

- A magazine reporter on McDougal: "McDougal is a totally unreliable witness."

- CBS's Scott Pelley on McDougal: "I found him not wholly credible... because of his eccentricities."

Others who spoke with Hale and/or McDougal found them somewhat more believable. Nonetheless, even a split decision on these two central Whitewater figures seems to put them well behind Jones and the troopers on a credibility scale. Yet, at the time the troopers' and Paula Jones's allegations were made public, the press bent over backwards to argue that these accusers were not credible.

4. THE CONSERVATIVE TAINT

When considering the accusations of both the troopers and Paula Jones, most journalists were turned off by the involvement of right-wing partisans in bringing the charges to the forefront. *Los Angeles Times* media writer Thomas Rosenstiel's comments concerning Troopergate were generally representative of his colleagues:

> The Troopergate story was originally tainted because it first appeared in the *American Spectator*, and the story in the *Spectator* was not good journalism. It was full of speculation, and basically printed any rumor that was passed on about Hillary Clinton.

The fact that the story appeared in a deeply conservative magazine, and also included some third-party accusations, allowed many in the press to dismiss it as an ideologically-motivated attack on the president. Yet many of the same charges were not treated much more seriously even when they were printed in the *Los Angeles Times*.

Similarly, reporters were properly skeptical of the Paula Jones allegations because they were originally voiced at the Conservative Political Action Committee convention with various renowned Clinton-haters (such as Cliff Jackson and Larry Nichols) present. Howard Kurtz of the *Washington Post* said of his paper's editors, "I'm sure they were put off by the partisan setting." As we have seen, however, reporters consistently received Whitewater tips from Floyd Brown's Citizens United, as well as from other diehard Clinton adversaries.

While reporters should obviously not accept any information received from partisan sources at face value, they can use these resources to assist in constructing their stories. Such *was* the case with Whitewater, but was *not* in the case of the sex stories. Not only is this inconsistent, but it ignores an obvious truth: just because allegations are promoted by conservative sponsors, they are not necessarily false or disqualified from public airing.

5. TROOPERGATE LACKED "LEGS"

One additional reason the media gave for quickly abandoning Troopergate is that the story seemed to have had nowhere to go beyond a piling on of repetitive allegations. In the parlance of journalism, the story had no "legs."

The original stories in the *American Spectator* and the *Los Angeles Times* were comprehensive. Had those stories simply alleged a few instances of infidelity, other news outlets *might* have followed up to determine if there was a pattern of this behavior on Clinton's part. Since the *Times* and *Spectator* articles offered enough examples to demonstrate that pattern, however, editors and producers at other outlets were disinclined to invest their limited resources simply to try to confirm or augment what had been previously reported.

In this respect, the media's approach to Whitewater was dramatically different. When reporters began examining the Clintons' financial records, subsidiary stories were produced in great abundance, from those about Hillary Rodham Clinton's commodities trading to the interwoven relationships among the business, legal and political communities of Little Rock.

Another missing "leg" for the personal stories was the GOP. The media are more likely to keep a story in the news if the political opposition is willing to seize upon it. While undoubtedly enjoying the president's distress, the vast majority of Republicans in Congress shied away from making either sex scandal a partisan football. This is in sharp contrast to the GOP's aggressive offensive plays on Whitewater. In fact, the drumbeat of Republican calls for congressional hearings helped create the frenzy over Whitewater in the early months of 1994.

Even without GOP help, Troopergate managed to grow one leg: the September 1993 phone call from the president to trooper Danny Ferguson. Many journalists soured on sex stories nonetheless saw this aspect of Troopergate as relevant and important. However, Ferguson's "phantom affidavit" crippled that leg, and the story quickly withered.

This instance is particularly notable when compared to the Whitewater-related coverage of George Stephanopoulos's phone call to Treasury officials over the hiring of Clinton critic Jay Stephens. The Stephanopoulos call dominated front pages and newscasts for several days, as well as producing *Time* magazine's sinister (and misleading) cropped cover picture of Stephanopoulos and the president in the Oval Office. Interestingly, the press elevated this story to the top of the front page even through Republican Congressman Jim Leach of Iowa termed Stephanopoulos's intervention "pretty natural."

6. THE CNN SIGNAL

A sixth factor facilitating the media's rapid withdrawal from coverage of Paula Corbin Jones is that her February 11 news conference was not carried on CNN. This may have assisted reporters and editors in ignoring Jones's allegations until the filing of her lawsuit. CNN's decisions to air or not to air events can often ratchet coverage up or down, by influencing the decisions of the other networks and many local stations. Just six weeks earlier, CNN had played a vital role in generating the media focus — however limited — on Troopergate. Fred Barnes of the *New Republic* suggested that,

> Troopergate would almost have been successfully submerged had it not been for CNN [running the story] on that Sunday [December 19, 1993]. That led other stations to go with it on Monday and Tuesday. Once that happened it was out [in public] completely.

CNN's airing of its interviews with the troopers prompted not just the national media but also the White House to take the allegations seriously. As we saw, the *Los Angeles Times* was awaiting a White House response before it would run its story. After CNN ran its Sunday piece, according to Bill Rempel:

> Then [White House official David] Gergen called Shelby [Coffey, Editor of the *Times*] and said "You've got our attention." This, of course, galled me to no end. CNN runs this and now we've got their attention? His point was since it was being treated seriously [on television] the White House was going to have to treat it seriously too, which of course is ridiculous. They should have been treating it seriously from the outset.

The key role CNN played in bringing Troopergate to the forefront, however temporarily, was not lost on the White House when the Paula Jones allegations emerged. CNN was contemplating covering the Jones news conference at the CPAC convention. But some sources claim White House senior advisor George Stephanopoulos called CNN President Tom Johnson and urged him not to cover the event.

This was not unusual; CNN's political editor Tom Hannon recalled that during the 1992 campaign, "Stephanopoulous would call constantly, even talking to the Headline News anchors if he didn't like the way stories had been reported." CNN Executive Vice President Ed Turner added, "Stephanopoulos made a career" of this. However, CNN's Vice President for Public Relations Steve Haworth responded, "Nobody remembers a specific call" from Stephanopoulos on the day of Jones's press conference, but "we don't deny that it might have happened, because he did call frequently." Haworth also explained that CNN did not air the Jones conference because "CNN did not have any independent knowledge of her on the plausibility of the charges."

Whether CNN's decision came about in part because of a Stephanopoulos call or not, the fact remains that the cable network made a critical decision not to carry Ms. Jones's press conference. Had they done so, it would have been much more difficult for other news organizations to avoid covering the story.

7. PAULA VS. ANITA: CLASS BIAS IN THE PRESS

A social class bias colored much of the coverage of Paula Jones after the filing of her lawsuit. On the talk show "Inside Washington," *Newsweek's* Washington Bureau Chief Evan Thomas referred to Jones as a woman "from a trailer park with big hair." An even more jarring example of journalistic "classicism" appeared in a *U.S. News* piece written by Lynn Rosellini about Jones's hometown:

> [Lonoke, Ark.] is the land of big hair and tight jeans with girls whose dreams soar no further than a stint at hairdresser's school, an early marriage and a baby named Brittany or Tiffany or Brooke.

Even one *U.S. News* staffer later admitted, "I think [it was] kind of elitist." And *U. S. News* editor Lee Rainie remarked, "If I could go back in time and scrub the piece one more time, I would probably have taken out some of the references and phrases that particularly set people off." These characterizations of Jones as she sought redress for alleged sexual harassment differed sharply from much of the media's treatment of Yale Law School graduate Anita Hill in her 1991 charges against Clarence Thomas. The Center for Media and Public Affairs calculated that Prof. Hill's personal coverage on the networks during the Thomas confirmation battle was 66 percent *positive* overall; as noted earlier, Ms. Jones's network coverage was 67 percent *negative*.

It is evident that the press collectively took Prof. Hill's charges much more seriously than Ms. Jones's. In addition to class bias, another explanation for the press's preference for Hill — and a commonly heard refrain among conservatives — was that the media's liberal bias was showing. As one national broadcast reporter surmised:

[There is] the feeling that sex stories are... distasteful, although there is a double standard to some extent because they didn't hear much handwringing about the coverage of the Anita Hill-Clarence Thomas thing... the feeling was [Thomas] is a sexual harasser, we better get after him... and this reflects, to some extent, a bias.

Yet the liberal leanings of much of the press do not necessarily carry over into the scandal coverage of President Clinton. Says the same reporter, "Personal sympathy for Bill Clinton [among the press] has evaporated if there ever was much of it." Indeed, many journalists testified to the current lack of warmth in the relationship between the president and the White House press corps. (See Sidebar E, pp. 91-96.)

Moreover, an ongoing content analysis of television's White House news, conducted by the Center for Media and Public Affairs, found that President Clinton received more negative coverage overall than President Bush had during the first 18 months of his administration. As a consequence, it is difficult to argue that the president has benefited much from a liberal tilt in coverage of these various scandal stories.

Similarly, conservatives have claimed the extended delay in the *Washington Post's* publication of its Paula Jones piece reflected political bias. One *Post* reporter responded that, "Everyone has their biases, [but] the argument [within the newspaper] was debated on other grounds. It was more, are we willing to print a very graphic sexual charge against *the* president, [rather than just] a liberal Democratic president." Moreover, the fact that the *Post* was the only news organization to undertake a thorough investigation of Jones's charges and ultimately printed a tough story belie suggestions that *Post* editors were trying to protect a president who shares their political views.

Finally, while class and political biases explain some of the disparity in the coverage of the Jones vs. Hill allegations, differing structural aspects of the two stories may have been a more decisive factor. Hill's charges came at a U.S. Senate confirmation hearing of a Supreme Court nominee — a completely legitimate and recognized forum with an essential public purpose. Jones's post-election charges were made in a non-official, ideological setting, and thus presented a stark contextual contrast.

* * * * * * * * * * *

In sum, then, several factors and rationales help explain the media's reluctance to cover Bill Clinton's alleged personal scandals: Many journalists, socially liberal by nature, are relatively unconcerned about sexual transgressions. Reportage about such matters is frowned upon in their profession, and by much of the public, as sleaze mongering or at least déclassé. The presidency is a special office, not lightly demeaned even by a highly critical press.

Moreover, there was a host of "easy exits," enabling news organizations to duck the unpleasant task of reporting these sleazy matters. The accusations supposedly were old news; the principals were motivated by greed, or were discredited as unbelievable; their charges were tainted by association with a virulently anti-Clinton crowd; and so on.

However much these factors help explain the media's approach (or aversion) to these stories, they do not necessarily justify the principle that non-reporting is good reporting. What lessons can be drawn from these conclusions? More importantly, what better alternatives for coverage of similar circumstances in the future are suggested by our findings?

- FOUR -

LESSONS AND PRESCRIPTIONS

Despite the increasing legitimacy of tabloid news, the mainstream media remain very uncomfortable about covering sex stories about the President of the United States. They ought to be hesitant, if only because the stakes are so high. Yet if substantial evidence is available of serious offenses, the available facts should be published or broadcast in a fair and thorough fashion. This did not always happen in 1993 and 1994, as we have just seen. Some news organizations virtually ignored the presidential sex stories, while others applied journalistic standards to these personal scandals that were not consistent with the way they cover other scandals.

Granted, this is a thorny and difficult area. Given the tenor of the times and the growth of the character issue, though, similar stories about public figures are probably inevitable, and the press needs to get it right. But how to do so?

A preliminary and necessary step is for the national press corps to recognize that stories about a presidential candidate's or a president's sexual transgressions can no longer be hidden from public view by a small number of media elites, as occurred in John F. Kennedy's era. The proliferation of news outlets and the public's concern about moral issues and values, among other factors, have changed the landscape dramatically and irrevocably in recent years. This evolution of media culture has at least two crucial implications.

First, journalism needs to come to better terms with character issues, and serious news organizations need to do so with standards that are thoughtful and mature. This means, for example, that news outlets cannot simply and categorically turn a blind eye to distasteful personal stories. Rather, each organization must decide for itself which sexual sins, and in what contexts, have relevance to a public official's candidacy or performance in office.

Second, it is particularly important for the mainstream media to confront these issues so that the stories are not defined only by tabloids, the ideological press, or radio talk shows. As Eleanor Clift of *Newsweek* noted about the Paula Jones accusations, "Because of our reluctance to talk about the Jones affair, we've given free license to Clinton's opponents, to the talk show hosts who are perfectly happy to talk about this and to embellish and put out their videos." By getting out in front on a story, the mainstream media can potentially report these allegations in a more balanced and careful manner.

Without taking the initiative on such stories, however, the national press will repeatedly find itself in the unenviable position of following the often smarmy lead of the tabloid press. As Bill Rempel of the *Los Angeles Times* said of his paper's decision to delay publishing the troopers' charges, "What we did was let [the *Spectator's*] right-wing, poorly done story get out there and become, in a sense, the story that [the *Los Angeles Times*] had to defend."

It will not be easy for the press to develop clearer, more rigorous standards for coverage of sexual matters. And it will always be difficult to achieve high-level, constructive public dialogue about them. Yet as Thomas Rosenstiel observed, journalists "have not progressed as we should have since Paul Taylor [of the *Washington Post*] asked Gary Hart about [adultery] in '87.... The press should have had an open discussion on this, but we haven't."

Options for Future Coverage

Past experience can point to possible solutions, partly by eliminating strategies that had undesirable effects. News organizations took a variety of approaches to the Clinton personal scandal stories, and the major outlets differed widely in the ways they covered or avoided them. In retrospect, which approaches best served readers and viewers?

THE "SEE NO EVIL" OPTION

CBS and NBC, most notably, did not even mention Paula Jones's February 11 news conference on their evening news broadcasts. Their primary justification was that they had no way of knowing whether her allegations could be substantiated. Obviously, this was true for all news organizations at the time, although reporters who had interviewed the Arkansas troopers were familiar with part of the story (Jones's meeting Clinton in a hotel room).

The problems with this approach are twofold. First, this was tantamount to pretending that the allegations did not exist, even though everyone in Washington, and many in the country, were talking about the story. Second, at the same time these organizations were saying they did not know the truth of her accusations, they were doing nothing to determine the truth.

THE MINIMALIST OPTION

The tactic employed by many news outlets was simply to note that the allegations had been made and then leave the story there. Among the networks, only ABC chose this route, and Brit Hume defended his employer's approach:

> There's a phenomenon in news coverage that has to do with a story that becomes so overwhelmingly evident to your audience that you have to deal with it because your audience expects you to.... After you report it, unless

something happens that furthers it in the way of news, you don't have to worry about it too much. You don't have to lead with it on your broadcast or put it on the front page of your paper, but you cover it.

Such an approach is clearly more defensible than ignoring the story altogether, since readers and viewers are at least informed of its existence. Nonetheless, it is a passive approach that leaves news consumers wondering about an allegation's validity.

THE INVESTIGATIVE APPROACH

Among the national media, only the *Washington Post* adopted this method with its decision to ignore Paula Jones's press conference but undertake an extensive investigation into her claims. The *Post's* approach can be criticized for its failure to say anything about the charges immediately, since this was close to telling its readers that nothing had happened the day before. The story also took too long, and its publication depended too much on an independent news peg (the hiring of Robert Bennett).

On the whole, though, this piece offered a balanced and comprehensive perspective on Ms. Jones's allegations, the closest to a model approach seen in this case. (See Sidebar B.) Thomas Rosenstiel, the *Los Angeles Times* media writer, called the *Post's* approach "a pretty fair way to cover the story, and basically the right way." Of course, not every news organization was going to initiate a multi-month investigation, but the Jones charges **should** have been taken seriously by more publications and broadcasts.

Categorizing Stories

While the approaches listed above pertain to how news organizations cover a story, the larger question involves the **relevance** of allegations about the president's personal life. Editors and reporters have varied greatly in evaluating the relevance of these allegations. Ultimately, individual outlets set their own policy, making any universal consensus unlikely. Nonetheless, news organizations ought to be able to draw distinctions among major categories of personal stories, and to establish a specific policy for each category.

In grappling with the president's personal behavior, many in the media have simplistically lumped Gennifer Flowers, Troopergate, and Paula Jones together under the heading of "sex stories." Yet each set of allegations is manifestly different, and deserves separate and thoughtful treatment. These cases illustrate three key distinctions that should shape coverage of such stories:

1. THE TIMING OF THE CHARGE

The first important aspect is the timing of the philandering charge. The relevance of the allegation is certainly greater during a campaign than afterwards, if only because many voters value this information and use it to influence their choice on election day. Assuming that credible evidence exists to support a charge of infidelity, the facts of the case should be published or broadcast promptly during a campaign.

2. COVERAGE COMMENSURATE WITH TRANSGRESSIONS

The extent of the coverage given to an infidelity charge should be strongly influenced by the extent of the candidate's transgression. A long-ago affair or a rare example of infidelity deserves perfunctory treatment, if coverage is necessary at all. Flagrant and repeated unfaithfulness to one's spouse demands more serious examination.

The *Washington Post's* Howard Kurtz pointed to Bill Clinton's potentially "compulsive" or "pathological" behavior as one of the most newsworthy aspects of the Troopergate story. Kurtz argued that Troopergate was news in part because of the "extent of [his indiscretions]. The sheer numbers, the frequency, the calls at one in the morning, frankly get your attention. I don't know if they make [up] a huge news story, but it does make a news story." Mr. Clinton's alleged pattern of personal promiscuity also revealed vital aspects of his approach to public policy, according to *Newsweek's* Joe Klein:

> Watching Clinton operate has changed my view about how we should deal with issues of personal propriety. I used to believe we had to cut [politicians] some slack. But the more I looked at Clinton's foreign and domestic policies, the more I saw his lack of discipline, the inability to commit, and the way he leads people on.... Indeed [Clinton's] ***public*** life has been marked by flagrant promiscuity, and therefore it raises the question of whether we should have looked more closely at the rest of his life.

3. WHEN SEX IS NOT THE WHOLE STORY

While sex will always soak up the headlines, non-sexual aspects of a story can completely justify the publication or airing of a "sex story."   These aspects certainly include the use of government employees to facilitate or cover up indiscretions, offers of government jobs for silence, or the use of the power of one's office to secure sexual favors, especially involving subordinate workers.

All of these aspects were in evidence to some degree in the Clinton personal life stories. It can be argued, in fact, that the sexual component was little more than an uncomfortable context for the real crux of Troopergate and Paula Jones.   As Bill Rempel of the *Los Angeles Times* said of Troopergate:

> This story is about abuse of office, when Clinton exchanged sexual favors for favors of the government (jobs, appointments) and used his troopers — state employees — to carry out and conceal these personal transactions. And this is also a story about deceit. He looked into the camera at the critical moment of his campaign for the [presidential] nomination and he told sixty million Ameri-

cans he did not have an affair with Gennifer Flowers. That was a lie. He lied to the public to get the nomination, he abused his office as governor, and then when he was in the presidency, he abused that office to try and keep the story from coming out by offering jobs-for-silence. Now that is classic, old-fashioned abuse of office, abuse of power, abuse of privilege.

Many journalists failed to see the troopers' allegations as anything different from the Gennifer Flowers claims, owing mainly to their squeamishness about stories with sexual content. Similarly, there were two aspects of the Paula Jones allegations that went beyond infidelity. The first involved sexual harassment, which made the Jones case different from any that came before. The second important facet of that story is her status as a state employee, over whom Clinton had at least indirect control.

While the question of harassment may forever remain unresolved in the netherworld of "he said/she said," most of the journalists interviewed for the book believe that Mr. Clinton and Ms. Jones were in the hotel room together at his instigation. Hence, even if the harassment charges are dismissed as unproven, journalists should have been interested in the obvious abuse of power aspect of the accusation.

By considering these factors separately and together, news organizations might be able to resolve some of their anxieties about stories of a personal nature. One lesson is clear: The media should avoid lumping all such stories into one nonreportable category.

Applications to the Clinton Sex Chronicles

Our extensive interviewing of reporters, editors, correspondents, and producers about their coverage of Mr. Clinton's personal life revealed a deep-seated ambivalence, if not outright resistance, concerning this task. "I didn't get into journalism to do this" was the most commonly heard refrain. Yet all agreed that some coverage of the personal lives of public figures is necessary if there is some reasonable connection to the individual's performance in public office. Relevance to public performance, then, may very well be the key consideration.

Some in the press corps have repeatedly suggested that the sex allegations against *Governor* Clinton, even if true, are irrelevant to *President* Clinton's conduct of office. But this view ignores several factors:

◆ It can be argued that the sexual episodes allegedly involving Bill Clinton, if true, would reveal significant character traits and attitudes that can affect the Clinton presidency, including:

- a pattern of extensive lying and cover-up;

- careless and selfish use of taxpayer money and resources, especially in the designation of public-salaried police guards as procurers of mistresses;

- arrogance in an apparent belief that the normal rules of social and political conduct do not apply;

- a recklessness in the pursuit of sex reminiscent of Mr. Clinton's political hero, John F. Kennedy;

- willingness to use the powers of office for personal gain;

- arguably, a kind of demeaning sexism that sees women — first and foremost — as mere objects of sexual desire and among the perks of high office;

- behavior that makes it difficult for a president to take up the cause of promoting so-called "family values," or to argue in the age of

AIDS against dangerous and self-destructive activities such as sexual promiscuity.

◆ If the troopers' reports are true — and, as indicated earlier, most journalists who have investigated them believe they are — they indicate compulsive behavior. Any compulsive activity is difficult to control, much less stop. The troopers claim Mr. Clinton demonstrated as much in continuing his infidelities even *after* the Gennifer Flowers frenzy nearly destroyed his presidential candidacy (and after he and Hillary Rodham Clinton claimed on "60 Minutes" that their marital troubles were in the past). Indeed, the troopers contend that Bill Clinton's Arkansas escapades extended through the 1992 election and right up to the eve of his inaugural. On January 20, 1993, of course, the Secret Service took control of the president's security.

◆ A governor's or president's private life, whenever it is messy and indiscreet, presents opportunities for untoward influence by those who have knowledge of the unflattering aspects. The threat of public disclosure, whether it is overt, implied, or unstated, opens up a leader to risks of subtle or blatant kinds of extortion.

The recent troubles that Secretary of Housing and Urban Development Henry Cisneros has encountered with a vindictive ex-mistress demonstrate that this issue is not merely hypothetical. There is no evidence that anything of the sort has happened to Clinton. But one national reporter who is familiar with the allegations about the president's private life bluntly observed: "I think Clinton may have opened himself up to blackmail."

◆ The press may believe the notion is naive — many scoff at it or don't even acknowledge it — but the president is a powerful role model for the nation, particularly for its youth. Some public opinion polls indicate that a majority of Americans claim not to care about philandering by public officials. Yet it is also undeniably true that a sizeable portion of the citizenry expects a certain decorum and high standards of behavior from the First Citizen.

Some journalists have insisted that Bill Clinton ought to be evaluated on his policies and accomplishments, not his private life weaknesses. *This may well be the correct view, but the American people should be the judge.* Whether or not reporters agree with their view, philandering matters to many voters. If the evidence of adultery is substantial, information about this dimension of candidates' or officeholders' lives ought to be provided to the American electorate — not withheld by a press corps whose perspectives on life-style issues often differ from those of the country's mainstream. And even citizens who object to reporting about marital infidelity emphatically agree that abuse of power or misuse of public resources is a fit subject for reporting.

These arguments are not new. In his 1991 book, *Feeding Frenzy: How Attack Journalism Has Transformed American Politics*, Larry Sabato suggested a "fairness doctrine" to draw the boundaries for responsible coverage of the private life of public officials. Many of them can be applied directly to the allegations leveled against the president by the troopers and Paula Jones, including the following:

PRIVATE LIFE SUBJECT TO PUBLICATION AND BROADCAST

- Any incident or charge that reaches the police blotter or a civil or criminal court.

- Sexual activity where there is a clear intersection between an official's public and private roles; for example, relationships with staff members or lobbyists, where elements of coercion or conflict of interest inherently exist.

- Sexual activity that is compulsive and/or manifestly indiscreet, and therefore potentially dangerous; for example, the cases of John Kennedy and Gary Hart.

- Any private behavior that involves the use of public funds or taxpayer-subsidized facilities in a substantial way.

- Offenses committed after a politician's declaration of candidacy, when any prudent individual will be on his or her best behavior. [These] are justifiably subject to added emphasis.

- A candidate's degree of... lying can also rachet coverage up....

* * * * * * * * * * * *

Just about everyone, journalist and non-journalist alike, agrees that these subjects are difficult and unpleasant, all the more so when they are raised in the midst of an officeholder's term. The early manifestations of the personal life issues now plaguing Bill Clinton's presidency should have been more fully, carefully, and thoughtfully explored during the 1992 presidential campaign. That they were not is a major failure of electoral journalism for which the country is still paying.

The unresolved Whitewater affair and the character issues surrounding Bill Clinton have resulted in "post-campaign campaign coverage," an extension of the 1992 election debate into Clinton's presidency itself. While one could contend that such day-late-and-dollar-short coverage is better late than never, these matters are undermining Clinton's governance and distracting both the president and the country from pressing policy concerns.

In retrospect, it is clear that the 1992 campaign press corps was spooked by the Gennifer Flowers affair. With no desire to repeat the Gary Hart-Donna Rice debacle, and revolted by the tabloidization of Flowers' charges, journalists resisted opportunities to probe the unanswered questions about Bill Clinton's personal life and associated issues such as the misuse of state personnel. As a result, the public was kept mostly in the dark and left to assume that Mr. Clinton's activities were not serious or had ceased.

Had the electorate been more fully informed, candidate Clinton might have truly been able to put the issue behind him and enter his presidency less encumbered. Or the voters might have made a different electoral decision, with Democrats nominating a "cleaner" candidate or the general electorate choosing one of the other presidential contenders.

Thus, the consequences of the media's inability to deal with the character issue in 1992 have been, and will continue to be, enormous. The incentives for journalists to do better next time ought to be even greater. If they are ever going to get it right, journalists will have to grapple with the character issue in a more sensible and systematic fashion. The current piecemeal approach, with its inevitable hypocrisies and inconsistencies, serves the interests of neither the president nor the American public nor the journalistic profession.

President Clinton's moral stature will be compromised so long as whispers of personal scandal follow him with no prospect of their being openly addressed and fully resolved. The electorate's apathy and cynicism towards public life are only increased by a vague sense that unpleasant matters are being withheld from them by a closed circle of political and media elites. And mainstream journalists are reduced to trading insider anecdotes, while their tabloid and talk show competitors keep stirring the pot with rumors and conspiracy theories that cry out for old-fashioned rigorous journalistic inquiry.

In short, the character issue is not going to fade away, and the tough calls will only become more taxing without a new and more intellectually defensible approach by the mainstream news media.

Sidebar A: *The Los Angeles Times*

It Was the Best of *Times*. It Was the Worst of *Times*.

In the second week of August 1993, *Los Angeles Times* reporter Bill Rempel had just returned from his honeymoon when he received a phone call from Arkansas attorney Cliff Jackson. Rempel knew Jackson was an outspoken antagonist of President Clinton and an instrumental actor in Clinton's draft controversy during the 1992 campaign. Now he was calling to tell Rempel that a friend of his, Lynn Davis, was representing some people who had a story they wanted to tell about Mr. Clinton's tenure as governor of Arkansas.

Without offering many details, Jackson told Rempel that the stories were related to Gennifer Flowers and other uncorroborated womanizing rumors that had swirled around Mr. Clinton's 1992 campaign. The *Times* decided that there would be no harm in sending Rempel to Arkansas to listen, ask some questions and determine if there was a news story there.

The people with the tales to tell in Arkansas turned out to be three state troopers who had been assigned to Governor Clinton's security detail. They related stories involving their roles in facilitating extramarital trysts on the part of the then-governor. (A fourth trooper also eventually served as a primary background source, with a number of other troopers providing corroborating information on an off-the-record basis.)

Very quickly Rempel realized that he finally had something he had searched for during an earlier stint in Little Rock from February until September, 1992: "What the troopers provided was a third-party witness to events we had heard about before. That was a level of corroboration unavailable" during the presidential campaign. Rempel found their testimony credible — it checked out. And, after all, as a reporter for the *Washington Post* would later tell us, "This information wasn't coming from indicted felons; it was coming from sworn law enforcement officers" who had had the closest possible access to Clinton over a long period of time.

Rempel worked on the story for four months, during which he was joined by Douglas Frantz of the *Times* Washington Bureau. Rempel got to know the troopers reasonably well, and he insists money "was not the motivating factor" for at least two of them. However, he admits that some of the troopers "hoped to get a book deal" and even asked him to write it. (He refused.)

Eventually the troopers accepted his ground rules: Some of them "would have to be on the record; they would receive no financial reward; they would have to provide great detail so that I could corroborate their claims with other people and documents to the extent possible." What the troopers did not tell Rempel at first is that they had also contacted David Brock of the *American Spectator*. When Rempel learned of this, he "expressed my displeasure... but it was too late." The competitive element had been introduced, and it would influence the development of the story at several points.

Those involved in the *Los Angeles Times* investigation note that many of the incidents told to Rempel and Frantz by the troopers were never published--not because they were necessarily inaccurate but because they could not be independently substantiated to a sufficient degree. One of those incidents was that of Paula Corbin Jones, though her name was not disclosed to the reporters. Danny Ferguson, the trooper who accompanied then-Paula Corbin to Clinton's hotel room in 1991, regaled Rempel with the details he knew about the encounter.

According to Ferguson, after Jones left, Clinton told him "he [Clinton] couldn't do anything so all they did was talk." To Ferguson and the other troopers that statement was ambiguous, since he claimed Clinton often "would come out of these sessions where everybody knew there was sex going on and say, 'Ah, we had a nice talk!'" To his later regret, Rempel did not pursue this story, forthrightly admitting that he "missed the point that this woman was someone Clinton had supervisory authority over [and that therefore] it met the standard of abuse of office."

By mid-December, after numerous interviews with the troopers and additional weeks of reviewing voluminous state records, Rempel and Frantz completed their reporting and were ready to produce the story that would come to be known as Troopergate. The *Los Angeles Times* eventually published the story on Tuesday, December 21, but the preceding week was filled with cautious decision-making and internal struggles over the piece. The result was that Troopergate was yesterday's news by the time it appeared in the *Times*.

The *American Spectator*, a conservative monthly, published a similar story that was released on Monday, December 20. In addition, CNN, having received an advance copy of the *Spectator* piece the previous Friday, interviewed the troopers and aired excerpts on Sunday, December 19. The *Los Angeles Times* article remained significant mainly for offering credibility to some of the allegations made in the *Spectator* story, which many journalists had dismissed as nothing more than an ideological attack. Nonetheless, after an extensive investigation and commitment of resources, the *Times* had lost its scoop.

The two *Los Angeles Times* reporters had tried to forestall such an outcome. On Monday, December 13, Rempel and Frantz had met with the *Times's* top editors in Los Angeles. They received the green light to go to Washington to present their findings first to *Times* editors and then to the White House for a response. After taking a red-eye flight from L.A. to Washington, the reporters went to the *Times's* Washington Bureau to present the story to Bureau Chief Jack Nelson and Deputy Dick Cooper.

Prior to this time, only the reporters and four other top editors at the paper knew that the Troopergate story was in the works. The reporters were working in Little Rock under the guise of covering Whitewater (which they did simultaneously).

The primary reason for the internal secrecy was the off-and-on reluctance of the troopers to make their allegations on the record. Said Rempel of the troopers, "They were like little boys on a high dive. They had gotten out there but they didn't know whether to take the jump or scramble back to the ladder and get out of there. It became an exercise for us to try to persuade them to go ahead, that this was a story of merit and importance to the country and they were the only ones in a position to do it." As a consequence the paper could not afford to risk any accidental leaks, since the story might easily have died. It took Rempel and Frantz until Thanksgiving of 1993 to get a final on-the-record commitment from the troopers.

The reporters showed Nelson and Cooper their memos on the story and affidavits from the troopers. (The story itself was not yet written.) As word gradually leaked out about the *Los Angeles Times* investigation, rumors spread among the Washington press corps that Nelson was vehemently opposed to printing the story and had threatened to resign if it was published. Nelson said of such rumors, "I never gave a recommendation one way or another whether the story should run... [and] the threat to resign never even crossed my mind."

Rempel remembers Nelson's initial response to be, "Hell of a story," although he recommended (with *Times* Editor Shelby Coffey's concurrence) that the troopers take polygraph tests, which they had offered to do in their affidavits. Rempel and Frantz were strongly opposed to what Rempel called "voodoo reporting," citing the scientific questionability of polygraphs. Nonetheless, an effort was made to heed Nelson's suggestion. The attempt was hamstrung, however, by Arkansas licensing requirements for polygraphers, which prevented the *Times* from importing their own tester. The paper also considered flying the troopers to a different state for the tests.

In the end, it proved to be logistically impossible to arrange on short notice. According to Rempel, "it would have added a couple of weeks to our reporting, which was by then impossible because the *Spectator* was coming out." (ABC News had also considered ordering polygraphs for the troopers, but ABC's correspondent for the story, Mike von Fremd, said he also "objected very strongly to that. I'd hate to get to the point where for every interview I do, I'd have to say, 'O.K., is the sound man ready? Do we have the lie detector in place?'" ABC also dropped the idea.)

On Thursday, December 16, the two reporters finally presented a list of questions to White House advisor David Gergen. The White House, however, was in no hurry to offer a response. The administration's stalling was a direct result of the policy adopted by the paper. As Rempel said, "We had adopted a position... that we were going to wait and not be rushed. We were not even going to rush the White House in responding. We weren't going to go out there and publish even if they did not respond; we were just going to sit there and wait."

Shelby Coffey defended his decision this way: "We decided not to be stampeded by any competitive pressures. We were dealing with sensitive material and felt that the White House should not get just a hurried hour-before deadline call for response. Also, most importantly, we had not made the decision to publish until we got the response."

In the meantime, pressure was growing on the *Times* to publish its story. Advance copies of the *Spectator's* expose were already floating around Washington. In addition, as word leaked out that the *Times* also had the story, conservatives began clamoring for the paper to publish. Regardless, Rempel noted the real pressure was coming internally: "The heat on getting published... wasn't coming from the *Spectator*. It was coming from Doug Frantz and Bill Rempel and we were getting louder and louder. We were making as much heat inside as you could possibly make."

Eventually, it was the CNN report on Sunday the 19th, rather than the *Los Angeles Times* request, that forced the White House to respond. Once the CNN report was aired, the White House invited Rempel and Frantz to come over for a response. Leaving "Santa Claus and twenty-five kids singing Christmas carols" at a party at Frantz's Washington home, the reporters arrived at the White House around 8 p.m. and spent almost three hours there. In that span they met with then-White House counsel Bernard Nussbaum, deputy counsel Joel Klein, a reportedly "enraged" senior advisor Bruce Lindsey and press secretary Dee Dee Myers.

Rempel called the process "a charade... they bought time, delved into our story and got to see the troopers' affidavits, then gave us a two-paragraph response that was identical to what they had given the Associated Press much earlier in the day." However, the story was at least ready to go into Monday morning's paper, making its publication simultaneous with the official release of the *Spectator*.

Nonetheless, Coffey decided to hold the story one more day, explaining, "Accuracy, not speed, was more important.... [Delaying] was a proper decision because the story was [still] being rewritten and polished up to deadline the next day [Monday]." With Coffey's new delay, an exasperated Frantz announced that he was resigning. He was talked out of it at that point by National Editor Mike Miller, although several months later Frantz did quit and moved to the *New York Times*. One staffer said of the unpopular Sunday night decision to wait another day, "Every editor up to [Coffey] had been pushing the green light for some time. This was not the two reporters just bucking a bunch of their editors."

Ironically, waiting another day still did not eliminate a major flaw in the final story. Three days after the *Times* story appeared, the *New York Times* reported that the two troopers who had spoken on the record had been involved in a 1990 auto insurance scheme. In the eyes of many in the media, this damaged the overall credibility of the troopers' allegations, even though some questioned the importance of the insurance matter, and the other troopers who served as sources were unaffected.

The *Los Angeles Times* was criticized for not uncovering this information in their lengthy investigation. As it happened, though, Rempel and Frantz *did* discover the information and included it in a sidebar on the troopers' backgrounds. The editors in Los Angeles, however, decided to incorporate that information into the main body of the story. Then, in one of the final edits, that information was somehow dropped. Said Rempel of that omission, "Under the pressure to get an interview with the White House and fighting to get the story in the paper... we didn't have the stamina apparently to keep alert, and we missed what was lost in the final version...   I don't believe it was consciously taken out as much as it was lost between the cracks in a big story." Apparently, the chief editor had lost sight of it completely. In September 1994, Shelby Coffey wrote to us, "I do not recall the 1990 insurance problems being in a sidebar."

In retrospect, Rempel expressed disappointment, not so much in his newspaper as in the rest of the media that "tried to discredit the story rather than report it." To Rempel, his article should have been taken more seriously because it was about "abuse of office and deceit: It is the kind of story the press ought to be aggressively pursuing, rather than running from or hiding or knocking down."

—co-authored by Thomas K. Hetlage

SIDEBAR B: *The Washington Post*

THE *POST* AND MS. JONES

On February 11, the day Paula Jones first publicly levied sexual harassment charges against President Clinton, editors at the *Washington Post* made a decision common to some other major news organizations: They agreed not to acknowledge her allegations in the next day's paper. But unlike other outlets that made a similar decision (e.g., NBC and CBS), the *Post's* editors determined that they would take the allegations seriously and examine them with an extensive investigation of their own. It seemed like a sound decision at the time, and indeed it proved superior to the paths chosen by other organizations. As a *Post* staffer retrospectively observed, though, that decision "proved to be a can of worms."

The *Post* sent a talented investigative reporter, Michael Isikoff, a second reporter from its soft-news "Style" section, and a photographer to cover Paula Jones's February news conference. Isikoff did some reporting that afternoon and wrote a brief story on the allegations. Senior editors decided not to run the story, however, because it was premised on accusations for which they had no proof and which were made in a highly partisan setting. (A brief dismissive mention of the Jones conference did run in "Style" three days later.) Rather, they resolved to undertake an independent investigation of Jones's charges because, as Assistant Managing Editor for National News Karen DeYoung put it, "From the start it was either a very minor bit of craziness, to be treated as such, or it was an extremely serious allegation." The *Post* decided to find out in which category the Jones matter fell.

Shortly after the news conference, Paula Jones and her handlers entered into a compact with Isikoff, agreeing to provide him exclusive access to both her and her relatives. Isikoff had interviewed Ms. Jones for three hours on the day after the press conference, and subsequently quizzed her several more times. He also travelled to Arkansas where, in addition to speaking with members of Jones's family, he interviewed Pam Blackard and Deborah Ballentine, the two women with whom she first talked after the alleged incident in 1991.

Isikoff said of Ballentine, with whom he met in person, and Blackard, with whom he spoke several times by telephone,

> [They] are enormously impressive and influenced me greatly in pushing for this....They struck me as highly credible, as people who did not have axes to grind in this. They were spontaneous, they were highly detailed and they were very up front. And they're not out seeking publicity. You can accuse Jones of that, but not these two.

One of Isikoff's regrets about the *Post* piece that was eventually published is that he "wish[es] more from Ballentine and Blackard had been in the story."

Most of Isikoff's reporting was completed by the end of February. Yet there was still much hand-wringing about what the *Post* could prove. As Isikoff admitted, "You can never prove something like this, and ultimately it comes down to his word against hers. But I thought that to the extent the story could be checked out, it did check out." A *Post* editor agreed that the paper "expended a huge amount of time, money, and resources to make sure the charge was as substantiated as humanly possible, although in the end it was still essentially one woman's charge against the President of the United States." Isikoff continued:

> One piece of unfinished business from Troopergate was the White House's question, 'If all this is true, where are the women?' O.K., here was a woman. Nobody really

doubted she was in the hotel room, alone with Clinton, even if people had questions about the sexual harassment charge. Since the White House denied all of it, at a minimum you had them on that [the Clinton-Jones meeting], and at a maximum you had a whole lot more.

Isikoff began pushing strongly to publish the story, while the paper's editors remained undecided. The debate culminated with a confrontation between Isikoff and National Editor Fred Barbash, with Barbash walking through the newsroom and Isikoff verbally hounding him from behind. An exasperated Barbash turned around to face the reporter, and the two engaged in a heated shouting match that was the talk of the *Post* staff for many weeks. The incident resulted in Isikoff's two-week suspension for insubordination.

Various conservatives seized on the confrontation and suspension as evidence that the *Post* was censoring a story damaging to Clinton. But the Isikoff-Barbash argument may have been more a product of bureaucratic infighting and a reporter's frustration in a high-stress environment. Not only had Barbash and Isikoff clashed previously, but questions had been raised about whether Isikoff had gone outside the normal chain of command to "shop the story over to [the] "Style" [section]... which was something for the editors, not a reporter, to decide." As one *Post* staffer analyzed it, "Isikoff is an aggressive reporter and certainly he was frustrated the process was taking so long. I'm sure by the same token that some of his editors were losing patience with him." Isikoff eventually resigned in mid-May 1994. He is now working as an investigative reporter at *Newsweek*.

Wholly apart from Isikoff, there was pressure on the *Post* to publish the Jones story. Reed Irvine of the conservative watchdog group Accuracy in Media purchased advertising space in the *Post* on April 4 to run an editorial entitled, "Who is Paula Jones and Why is the *Post* Suppressing Her Charge of Sexual Harassment?" Two weeks later, on April 19, a similar ad was placed on the op-ed page of the *New York Times*. Journalists around Washington were also paying attention to the developments at the *Post*.   As Greg Ferguson of *U. S. News & World Report* recalled, Isikoff's suspension "was very widely talked about, not only at *U.S. News*, but among all other reporters I know."

In late February two other reporters, Sharon LaFraniere and Charles Shepard, were assigned to the story because some *Post* editors were not completely satisfied with Isikoff's work. They were particularly concerned over what one editor called Isikoff's "suggestive questioning" and the lack of detailed notes.

The new reporters were asked to double-check every aspect of the explosive exposé. According to Marilyn Thompson, one of the editors involved, they carefully retraced the steps described by Paula Jones, even "checking out [details of the] hotel room — almost like police work." They also reinterviewed Ms. Jones and several of the troopers. Thompson described the questioning as so "excruciatingly detailed" that an unhappy Paula Jones plaintively asked her interogator, "Why don't you believe me?"

Another staffer revealed that the *Post* even tried to identify and contact two dozen reputed Clinton paramours to see whether other women who might have refused his advances were subjected to the same kind of treatment, such as grabbing and exposure. The *Post* discovered no similar cases, although a *Post* reporter noted that Clinton may have been "in a position where he didn't get turned down very often. Most of the time it was consensual and there was no rancor."

After lengthy discussion, *Post* editors decided not to include information about the other women in the Jones story, primarily because it would have been "mixing apples and oranges." One other dead end for the *Post* reporters was Trooper Danny Ferguson, who refused to be interviewed despite repeated entreaties by staffers on the scene in Little Rock. Nor would the White House cooperate. "We got lots of off-the-record responses," remembered one staffer, but no official White House comment was ever forthcoming.

Eventually, the Jones saga was published under the three reporters' bylines on May 4. This effectively ended the argument that the *Post* was suppressing the story. Nonetheless, as many suspected at the time, a great deal of internal debate and worrying took place at the *Post* before the article was published.

The apparent catalyst for the publication of the story was the president's hiring of high-powered attorney Robert Bennett. The paper's editors were reluctant to run the story on its own, but preferred to use it in conjunction with a "real news" development. Bennett's hiring provided that development by signaling that the White House was treating the charges seriously. Some at the paper believe that the story would never have run without the hiring of Bennett or another significant external development, although senior editors dispute this. "Our backup plan was to work Jones into the broader context of Clinton's treatment of women," said one staffer.

Post employees also confirm that Managing Editor Robert Kaiser was "strongly opposed" to printing the story "the whole way through," whatever news pegs became available. In an internal memo to Executive Editor Leonard Downie, Kaiser expressed his discomfort with the fact that they still did not know with certainty whether the allegations were true. He also questioned whether the charges, even if valid, were relevant to Clinton's presidency.

The memo cited Kaiser's conversation with David Maraniss, a *Post* reporter who had closely studied Clinton's life for the newspaper and his own book project. Maraniss did not believe that Jones's claim of exposure was credible. "In the end [Kaiser's objections] didn't matter," notes Marilyn Thompson. But she and others defend Kaiser's role in the process as a useful one: "The atmosphere of the *Post* is one that encourages debate about everything... and Kaiser is a leader of that academic approach to journalism." Adds Sharon LaFraniere, "There have been debates about stories where I'm glad no one was there taking notes, but on this I was proud of the way we handled it."

The debate in the *Post* newsroom over Paula Jones and related matters may not be over. Said Assistant Managing Editor Karen DeYoung in September 1994: "I still don't consider it a dead story."

—co-authored by Thomas K. Hetlage

SIDEBAR C
TROOPER L. D. BROWN:
THE FORGOTTEN TROOPER

When the December 1993 *American Spectator* printed David Brock's Troopergate story, "Life With the Clintons," the national spotlight shone brightly on the author. This was not Brock's debut on the political stage. Earlier that year he had published a controversial book, *The Real Anita Hill,* which challenged Hill's 1990 sexual harassment allegations against Supreme Court nominee Clarence Thomas. At that time Brock was condemned by liberals and championed by conservatives in a polarized debate that was rekindled following the Troopergate story.

The *Washington Post* profiled Brock on the front page of its "Style" section. Frank Rich of the *New York Times* attacked Brock in a column, calling him "a smear artist... whose motives are at least as twisted as his facts." *Newsweek* said of Brock in its "Conventional Wisdom" column, "*American Spectator* 'journalist' swallows any pond scum that fits his right-wing agenda." Whether being lambasted by other "journalists" or championed on the Rush Limbaugh show, David Brock became a news story of his own and even something of a household name, at least in households metaphorically located inside the Beltway.

No one could say the same about another investigative journalist at the *Spectator*, Daniel Wattenberg (the son of PBS's "Think Tank" host Ben Wattenberg). It probably has not bothered Daniel Wattenberg that he missed the brickbats thrown at colleague Brock over Troopergate. But he might well have wanted to show up on Washington's radar screen after he wrote a highly-charged *Spectator* piece in the April/May 1994 issue that offered additional detailed allegations involving Bill Clinton's personal life in Arkansas. In contrast to the major splash caused by Brock's piece, the Wattenberg story generated barely a ripple in the Potomac. From the White House to the pressrooms and broadcast studios, Washington simply ignored it.

Wattenberg's article, "Love and Hate in Arkansas: L. D. Brown's Story," focused on the allegations of L.D. Brown, an Arkansas state trooper and Clinton bodyguard. Brown was particularly close to the then-governor before a 1985 falling out. His detailed accusations supported in a variety of ways the claims of the four troopers cited in the *Spectator's* and the *Los Angeles Times's* original Troopergate stories. Brown offered more alleged instances of the governor's use of his state-employed bodyguards to solicit and procure women. He also described reprisals by the governor after Brown ceased being Clinton's fair-haired trooper. Finally, the article gave further testimony about White House efforts to quiet Clinton's former bodyguards.

The Wattenberg story earned only a modicum of attention from the mainstream press. Not surprisingly, the *Washington Times* summarized Brown's claims in a front page story. But the *Washington Post* only ran a short article inside the front section, referring to "Decades-Old Allegations." No other major news organization even acknowledged Brown or Wattenberg, apparently considering the "new" article just more of the same following Brock's opus.

Yet the story behind the story in Wattenberg's case was no mere carbon copy. It began with a call to the *Spectator* from Joyce Miller, a college English instructor in Texas, in the aftermath of Troopergate. She claimed to have been propositioned on behalf of the governor by one of Clinton's bodyguards at a dance in the mid-1980's. As documentation, she provided Wattenberg with a photocopy of the business card the trooper had boldly left with her. The name on the card was L. D. Brown.

Wattenberg contacted Brown, whose first response was, "Oh, s--t." Brown said he did not remember the incident with Miller, adding, "But my God, it was so many times. I mean, good grief." The fact that Brown did not initiate his allegations certainly added to his credibility, and it was one key element of the Wattenberg story that differed greatly from Brock's original Troopergate scoop. As Wattenberg argued, "When [Brock's] story came out, the chief line of attack by the critics was to say, 'Oh, these guys are puppets of Cliff Jackson'.... Then I came out with a story with similar kinds of information from someone who was completely unconnected to Cliff Jackson and... they sort of ignored that fact."

Wattenberg said that Brown was initially reluctant to reveal what he knew, because he feared reprisal: "A lot of the good sources in Arkansas are afraid of the Clinton political machine." Wattenberg added, "Once word filtered back to the Clinton loyalists that Brown was talking to me, he [Brown] started receiving vague threats." The press, he said, "has only focused on the *incentives* for the troopers to talk, with virtually no attention at all to the *disincentives*, from exposing possible criminal conduct of their own to the fear of ostracism."

Certainly a major reason for the mainstream media's lack of interest in the L. D. Brown story was the reluctance to resurrect an embarrassing subject they had buried in December 1993. Nonetheless, it can be argued that Brown substantially strengthened the original allegations with his detailed recollections of Governor Clinton's womanizing, including escapades during a variety of out-of-town trips on which Brown accompanied the governor. Wattenberg claims that well-hidden, warehoused state travel records, which Brown at the time did not think still existed, confirmed many of the facts Brown recalled about the trips. Also, by the time Brown's allegations were published, President Clinton had called the earlier trooper claims "outrageous" and "not so." Brown's accounts therefore added weight to the suspicion that the president had lied.

Brown's revelations to Wattenberg did not represent the first time he had told these amorality tales. He (and other troopers) had contemporaneously related many of the same incidents to others. Brown had also provided some of the derogatory information to Sheffield Nelson, Mr. Clinton's 1990 Republican gubernatorial opponent. Moreover, troopers had briefed Jim Guy Tucker when Tucker was considering a 1990 Democratic primary challenge to Clinton. Elected lieutenant governor instead, Tucker succeeded Clinton as governor in January 1993 when the governor, then president-elect, resigned.

L. D. Brown himself was no saint. He admitted to Wattenberg that he was the beneficiary of "residuals" from helping to engineer Clinton's alleged exploits. Wattenberg quoted Brown as saying, "Whatever [women were] left over, if you were so inclined, because you were with [Clinton], you had a real good shot at doing something [having sex] yourself."

In addition, Brown had a personal grudge against Clinton that clearly motivated him to embarrass the president. Brown, a former president of the Arkansas State Troopers Association, claimed that Clinton helped to engineer the end of his tenure as head of the group in 1989 by urging Roger Perry (ironically, one of the troopers who later made the first allegations against Clinton) to run against him. Subsequently, Brown decided not to seek reelection. Although he could provide no documentation, Brown also alleged (as did Perry and Larry Patterson) that Clinton then tried to "polish off his wounded enemy" by pressing for a criminal investigation of Brown's management of the association. Prosecutors investigated Brown's tenure but dropped the case for lack of evidence.

Perhaps the most newsworthy elements of Brown's story were the alleged attempts of Clinton operatives to pressure him not to reveal what he knew. Brown said that a Clinton campaign worker, whom he had known when she lived in Arkansas some years before, approached him in a bar in the summer of 1992. She inquired whether he was going to talk publicly about the Democratic presidential nominee's past. Brown stated that he would not do so, and that he just wanted to be left alone. Brown alleged that the woman then asked, "Well, what is it that you want?," to which he replied, "I don't want a goddamn thing."

Brown claimed that he surreptitiously followed the woman out of the bar and watched as she drove to a spot a block away. The woman pulled up to a parked car, from which former Clinton gubernatorial chief of staff Betsey Wright emerged. Brown drove past the two and shouted, "Hello, Betsey." (By her own account, Wright was deeply involved in the effort to prevent, in her words, "bimbo eruptions" during Mr. Clinton's 1992 campaign. She has also helped the Clinton White House cope with allegations of personal scandal.) Finally, Brown alleged that early in 1994, after the White House learned that he was speaking to the *Spectator*, a top Clinton aide (whom he would not name) called him with this threat: "How would you like your credit-card receipts splashed across the front pages of the newspaper?"

Since Brown's story appeared in the *Spectator*, according to Wattenberg, Brown has been demoted from a prestigious position in the special investigations unit in charge of white-collar crime to uniform duty "on the Highway Patrol writing speeding tickets" for the first time in over a decade. In September 1994, Brown filed suit against Arkansas Governor Tucker, claiming the demotion resulted directly from his allegations in the *Spectator*.

In retrospect, it almost did not matter what L. D. Brown had to say, as far as the mainstream media were concerned. They had already buried Troopergate, declaring it irrelevant or unproven. They were not going to give attention to any article on this shunned subject appearing in a right-wing magazine most had earlier roundly condemned. Further, by April of 1994 the major news organizations were in the thick of Whitewater, a relatively classy, Pulitzer-material scandal that required no apologies to cover.

Brown's tales may resurface in 1996, however, when Bill Clinton will presumably be running for a second term as president. Some of the most colorful anecdotes have yet to be published. Several major avenues of corruption Brown privately alleged have not yet been explored. Reporters whom we interviewed suggested Brown has purposely withheld considerable information, possibly as an insurance policy against trouble from those threatening him. The forgotten trooper may not be forgotten forever.

—co-authored by David H. Kaefer

SIDEBAR D: *The Washington Times*

TIMES ARE TOUGH... ON THE CLINTONS

Some would say that the *Washington Times* coverage of President Clinton's personal life has demonstrated the paper's conservative bias. Others would argue that the *Times* has simply challenged the president more than the liberal press. Regardless of one's perspective, it is clear that the *Washington Times's* focus on Whitewater and the personal stories involving the president has been markedly different than that of its mainstream competitors.

The *Times* has devoted far and away the most attention to the various scandal allegations. Fully 289 Whitewater-related stories were carried by the *Times* between November 1993 and mid-August 1994. That figure compares to 228 Whitewater-related stories printed during the same period by its cross-town rival, the *Washington Post*; 220 for the *New York Times*; and 170 for the *Los Angeles Times*. (See Graph 5, p. 116.) The disparity is even greater when the placement of stories is examined. Nearly 70 percent (199) of the *Times'* Whitewater articles appeared on the front page. By contrast, the *Post*, *New York Times*, and *Los Angeles Times* all had fewer than one-third of their Whitewater-related stories on the first page.

The kinds of stories gaining front-page billing in the *Washington Times* were also distinctive. The *Times* printed 112 stories that focused on congressional calls for hearings about Whitewater, as well as the hearings themselves. This was nearly double the number run by any of the other major papers. Of these 112 articles, more than two-thirds (78) were placed on the front page. None of the other papers placed more than half of these stories up front.

Commenting on these findings, *Times* Assistant Managing Editor Francis Coombs suggested that, "A newspaper reveals the things it's interested in with how it plays a story. We have played Whitewater consistently on the front page [because] we consider it an important story." Coombs also contended that, particularly with its early scoops on Whitewater, the *Times* was compensating for an overly pro-Clinton press: "A lot of the press was uncomfortable writing anything really hard-hitting about President and Mrs. Clinton; [for a long time] the Clintons were the darlings of the media elite."

The *Times* has also outdone its competitors in the headline category. Their tone is consistently critical of the Clintons, sometimes ominously so, as these examples indicate:

- "Leach Cites 'Milkenesque' Scent in Unfolding Whitewater Inquiry" (2/1/94, A1);

- "Questions Cloud Ruling of Suicide in Foster's Death: Autopsy Report Still Not Released" (1/28/94, A1);

- "Whitewatergate: Observers Note Nixonian Twists" (3/7/94, A1).

The *Times's* spin on a particular day's big news story also often differed from other newspapers. The *Times* had a tendency to see Mr. Clinton's glass as half empty when competitors saw it as half full. For instance, after the White House released the Clintons' tax returns for 1978-79 in March, readers of the *Times* read that "Clinton Tax Papers Lack Support for the Deductions," the latter referring to the president's claim of adjusted losses of $47,000. But readers who picked up the *Washington Post* the same morning would have learned that "Tax Records Back Clinton Account."

Ever since Whitewater and Bill Clinton's personal life became headline news, the *Times* has also given singular slants to the same events reported by other papers. In the aftermath of the original Troopergate stories, for instance, when the *New York Times* challenged the credibility of two troopers by describing their role in a 1990 auto insurance scam, the *Post* and *Los Angeles Times* picked up the *Times* story the next day. The *Washington Times* mentioned the information only in passing in its own article, focusing instead on White House attempts to discredit Clinton's accusers. Yet the *Times* ran a front-page story on December 24, 1993 challenging the credibility of Clinton-defender Buddy Young, another former bodyguard who had attempted to refute the other troopers' charges. The *Times* reported that in a 1990 trial at which he was a witness, the judge stated that Young had "a reckless disregard for the truth." None of the other major newspapers carried that information.

Perhaps the most obvious contrast between the *Washington Times* and its rivals, however, is the manner in which the various outlets referred to Hillary Rodham Clinton. While most news organizations used the traditional "Mrs. Clinton" or "the First Lady," the *Times* often ran headlines referring simply to "Hillary." Some may view this as disrespectful, but the *Times's* readership doubtless approved.

—co-authored by Thomas K. Hetlage

HEADLINE NEWS:

The *Washington Times* Versus the Competition

"President Stops Short of Denying Stories of Trysts"
--(*Washington Times*, 12/23/93, A1)

"President Denies Any Wrongdoing"
--(*Washington Post*, 12/23/93, A1)

"Readers Demand More Details of
Clinton Sex Stories"
--(*Washington Times*, 12/22/93, A16)

"Whitewater Probe Sparks Little Public Interest,
Survey Finds" (Story also says the same about Troopergate)
--(*Los Angeles Times*, 1/15/94, A4)

"Hale to Detail Clinton's Role in Whitewater; Ex-
Judge Strikes Plea Deal With Fiske"
--(*Washington Times*, 3/21/94, A1)

"Former Judge, Accused of Fraud, Tries to
Implicate Clinton; He Reportedly Promises He Will
Tell of President's Whitewater Role; White House
Discounts Charges by David Hale"
--(*Los Angeles Times*, 3/21/94, A1)

"Clinton Tax Papers Lack Support for Deductions"
--(*Washington Times*, 3/26/94, A1)

"Tax Records Back Clinton Account"
--(*Washington Post*, 3/26/94, A1)

"Another Trooper Says He Found Women
For Clinton; Spectator Describes a
Hillary-Foster Romance"
--(*Washington Times*, 4/12/94, A3)

"Decade-Old Allegation Against Clinton Reported;
Trooper Says He Recruited Women For Trysts"
--(*Washington Post*, 4/11/94, A6)

Sidebar E:

The Half-Truth and Nothing but the Half-Truth: The White House Credibility Gap Revisited

The Clinton White House has a major problem with the Washington press corps. This has little to do with the firing of journalists' favorite staffers in the travel office or restrictions on press access to the communications office. The problem is that many members of the Washington media simply do not believe much of what they hear from the president and his staff.

Says one prominent national reporter, "The Clintons are almost pathological in their secrecy. Clinton lies a lot." Another Washington editor surmised, "The White House seems to believe that if they say something enough it's true."

On the national level, Mr. Clinton's credibility questions first arose during the 1992 Democratic primaries when his less than straightforward responses to the Gennifer Flowers and draft controversies renewed his Arkansas-conferred moniker of "Slick Willie." For example, Jim Wooten of ABC said of the draft story, "I know the president as a candidate lied to me. He lied right to my face." From most reporters' standpoint, candidate Clinton's dissembling has carried over into his presidency. As *Newsweek's* Eleanor Clift said, "With Clinton it's sort of a search to see where he left himself an escape hatch...."

One reporter who has covered Whitewater extensively said that he noticed this pattern in the president's response to questions about meeting David Hale. The president originally stated that "he didn't recollect a meeting." Later Mr. Clinton offered a firm "no" when asked if he had ever met with Hale. Said the reporter, "I'm a big believer that the first time around [to ask a question] is the best time around. Clinton is a smart guy and a lawyer and he understands as well as anyone the meaning of the response 'I don't have a recollection,' as opposed to 'It never happened.' And [the latter] was the carefully crafted response [that emerged only] after many days of back and forth deliberation." Similarly, Mr. Clinton said he could not "recall" meeting Paula Jones, and one of his first comments about the troopers' stories was that they were "not so." These phrases could be construed as allowing for the tales to be substantially true but with some portions inaccurate.

In addition to the strategic half-denials, the White House has also developed a reputation with many reporters for not disclosing all they know about a story. The unintended effect has often been to extend the life of a controversy, as new details slowly emerge. A reporter working on the story about Hillary Rodham Clinton's commodities trading pointed to a clear example of this phenomenon. The reporter had requested access to various records in the case, but the White House's representative, who was in possession of the trading records and tax returns,

> refused to let me look at the tax returns and only let me look at the trading records very briefly, with no notes and no time to be able to understand them. If I had [been able to review them thoroughly], I would have been able to say in the first article what eventually came out in later articles, that Mrs. Clinton put down $1,000 and made $100,000.

Instead, the controversy flared anew when that information was later revealed. Ironically, this occurred as a result of a flawed piece of journalism. *Newsweek* claimed in its April 4 issue that the First Lady had not invested a dime to produce her windfall, misconstruing analysis from a source familiar with the tax returns and trading records. The source quickly disavowed the claim, and the magazine was forced to run a lengthy correction the following week. Nonetheless, as one reporter said of the story, "It smoked them [the White House] out," in that they were forced to release records to demonstrate that the First Lady had made at least a minimal initial investment. Yet the process was unnecessarily drawn out over more than a month. If the White House had simply released the records, the story might have disappeared in a few days.

Part of the problem stems from Mr. Clinton's White House aides, according to the journalists we interviewed. NBC's Lisa Myers had one notable experience with senior Clinton advisor Bruce Lindsey. NBC had run a piece suggesting that one loan Mr. Clinton had taken out while governor was personal in nature and not part of Whitewater, even though it was included in the $69,000 the Clintons originally claimed to have lost in the land deal. According to Myers, Lindsey returned her call and

> claimed to have a document in front of him showing that the loan... was in fact related to Whitewater. I kept saying to him, 'Isn't there some way you can give me that document off the record? I have no desire to put something on the air that isn't accurate'.... Well, of course, the president went on national television later and said he had forgotten that he had really borrowed that money as a down payment for a house for his mother.... Obviously the document that [Lindsey] claimed existed did not.

Whether the source is the president or his aides, the Clinton White House has not been well served by too-clever-by-half answers, which have stoked the media's frenzy over Whitewater in particular. One network correspondent put the case bluntly: "Reporters like Whitewater because they have a clear sense that the White House and Bill Clinton are lying to them." Agreed a newsmagazine reporter: "The Clintons have been acting all along like they're hiding something. That makes the press dig more."

According to one network correspondent, the media's distrust of White House answers on Whitewater could be traced back to the fall of 1993:

> When they really compounded the [Whitewater] problems was when we found out months later that they had been lying to us in October and were fully aware of the criminal referral from the Resolution Trust Corporation. This made liars out of at least two members of the president's staff with whom I had spoken.

NBC White House correspondent Jim Miklaszewski concurred and assessed the lasting damage to presidential-press relations:

> If you go back and look at everything that was said about Whitewater and Whitewater-related events, including the First Lady's commodities investment and the handling of Whitewater documents in Vince Foster's office, the story continued to change as each new fact was revealed. It appeared to many reporters at the White House that the truth in the Clinton White House was a moving target. Any reporter who is told one thing one day, and another the next, starts to become a little suspicious of what's going on.

> This White House, claiming all along that they had nothing to cover up, did everything to make it appear that they were covering up. Whether there was something to hide or whether it was simply bad management is yet to be determined. When you hear phrases from senior White House officials such as "That statement is no longer operative" — and I was in that briefing — everyone looks at each other and says, "Wait a minute, that came straight out of Watergate." Nobody thinks this is Watergate, of course, but these people are acting like it is.

The White House complains that the media are cynical and we refuse to take them at their word, [but] the White House hierarchy has only themselves to blame because they set an early pattern of not only not being forthcoming but of being misleading. Once you lose somebody's trust, especially the media's, it becomes very difficult, if not impossible, to win it back. I'm afraid that this administration is going to be stuck with that problem. When they tell us something is white, we're going to think it's black.

While the vast majority of the Washington journalists we interviewed are skeptical about the responses they receive from the current White House, they differ on how the Clinton administration compares with its immediate predecessors. ABC's Jim Wooten, a veteran observer of many presidencies, remarked that in his experience, "All politicians lie... so it's not like we're discovering the wheel" with Clinton. And NBC's Andrea Mitchell observed that the current administration's attitude towards the truth is not unique in her career: "It is comparable to what I experienced in the Reagan White House over the Iran-contra scandal." But one of her television colleagues sharply disagreed, insisting, "This White House lies more than any other I have covered."

Sidebar F:

Old Lessons Re-Learned

One of the wonders of Washington is that the players are forever retaking Public Relations 101, learning anew the lessons taught about the care and feeding of the press by every scandal since Watergate.

If avoiding bad coverage is the objective, the two paramount rules of the game are full, quick disclosure and truthfulness. Neither has been the strong suit of the Clinton administration, and their press relations have suffered accordingly. Time and again, administration officials have increased and extended their bad publicity by allowing the facts to dribble out over the months, frequently contradicting earlier explanations. Included in this category were:

- The saga of Vincent Foster's Whitewater files taken from his office after his suicide. A year after the fact, the White House contradicted earlier denials by admitting some of the papers were kept in the White House residence before being transferred to the Clintons' attorney.

- Deputy Treasury Secretary Roger C. Altman's dealings with the White House about Whitewater. Contrary to Altman's February 1994 testimony to the Senate Banking Committee that he had "only one substantive contact" with the White House, he actually had many. White House officials had also misled reporters about the subjects covered in a key meeting Altman had with them about the Madison Guaranty Savings and Loan investigation.

- Hillary Clinton's commodities trading. After refusing to disclose the size of Mrs. Clinton's original investment that yielded a profit of nearly $100,000, the White House finally revealed it to be $1,000. This came about in response to *Newsweek's* incorrect claim that she put no money at all into the deal. The early explanation that Mrs. Clinton personally made trading decisions after reading the *Wall Street Journal* also fell by the wayside. The Clintons' political and personal ally, James Blair of Tyson Foods, actually handled the account and arranged the trades.

Partly because of their unease with the subject of sex, reporters have been less willing to jump on White House attempts to delay, dodge, and deny the personal stories. For instance, after the troopers' allegations were published, the normally eloquent president responded to a direct question about the charges by saying, "We... we did, if, the, the, I, I, the stories are just as they've been said. They're outrageous, and they're not so." The rest of Mr. Clinton's team did little better. One national reporter summed up the overall White House response to Troopergate this way: "It was never clear... whether they were arguing that this doesn't matter, or whether they were arguing it is all false, or maybe some of it's true but it doesn't matter." Yet the same press corps that pounced on every Whitewater half-truth chose not to highlight the ambiguity in equivocal Trooopergate responses.

This situation may change as we move into the 1996 political season, when Clinton's opponents will presumably wage a no-holds-barred effort to deny him a second term. In such a heated political environment, the press is likely to revisit the sexual allegations. Then, Mr. Clinton's earlier efforts at denial could result in more critical coverage. Such stories are often transmuted from lurid sex tales into high-toned tests of a candidate's veracity.

In fairness, the White House has not stood alone in its resistance to learning the lessons of scandals past. Their antagonists have ignored the fate of some earlier accusers as well. Those relative innocents who step into the media spotlight tend to forget they can easily be devoured by a hungry press, especially if they leave themselves open to ruin. Let the accusers beware: If they can be discredited, they will be, since the powerful people they challenge will find their skeletons and deliver them to the news media.

Arkansas troopers Patterson and Perry would have been better served by disclosing their own records, warts and all, at the time of their original revelations. As the *Los Angeles Times*'s Bill Rempel explained months before they went public, "I told them what a media circus does to people.... I bluntly told them they were going to have their characters attacked [and] everything about their motives and background would be used against them." Similarly, Paula Jones, and her advisers were foolish to go public at a conservative conference. This inevitably tainted her claims with ideological bias and gave the press a reason to disregard or downplay the charges.

One conclusion is clear: Public relations refresher courses need to be offered regularly to all sides in Washington scandal stories.

Sidebar G:

Sex Please — We're British!
Clinton's Press Across the Pond

Americans are forthright and the English shy, according to the cultural stereotypes. But this typecasting has been turned on its head by press coverage of the president's personal affairs. While news organizations in the United States downplayed or ignored the sex allegations, the British press reveled in them and trumpeted every new detail. From the trashiest tabloid to *The Times of London*, Troopergate and Paula Jones were big news. As the accompanying table shows, some of the most lurid headlines have concerned purported Clinton paramours whose tales have received little or no attention in the American press.

The British papers usually recycled or expanded upon incidents contained in the *American Spectator* or *Los Angeles Times* pieces, securing photographs and background interviews on various women Clinton had allegedly dated. One woman, a former Arkansas beauty queen named Sally Perdue, had briefly surfaced during the 1992 presidential campaign to claim a 1983 affair with Clinton. Perdue disclosed racy new details of her alleged relationship with the then-governor to several U.K. publications in January 1994. They included titillating revelations such as Mr. Clinton's supposed wearing of a "slinky black nightgown" in her apartment, and a claim that she was threatened with violence if she did not keep his misdeeds from the press. Another Arkansas woman who received very frequent and lengthy telephone calls from Governor Clinton in 1989 and 1990 also achieved tabloid stardom, though unwillingly. (She vehemently denied any suggestion of an affair.)

Little of this material was printed or broadcast on this side of the Atlantic. The *New York Daily News* thoroughly reported Perdue's allegations on January 24 in a dispatch from London, and a few other papers (including the *Washington Times* and the *Wall Street Journal* editorial page) included bits and pieces. NBC apparently had a session with Perdue but decided against airing anything. Howard Kurtz of the *Washington Post* also wrote an extended and critical review of the British performance on the Clinton scandals for his paper's "Style" section on May 3.

Only once did a British newspaper beat its American counterparts into print about an imminent development in the Clinton scandal saga. Geordie Greig, American correspondent for *The Times of London*, broke the story of Paula Jones's intention to sue President Clinton for sexual harassment on May 1, two days before the suit became front-page news across America. Greig's dispatch produced a banner headline just below the masthead of the *Sunday Times*. Much of the second page was taken up with another Greig article about "the mounting toll of Clinton's women." The headline would have been far too daring for the *Times* of old, but it seemed to fit perfectly both the scandal and the paper's need to compete in today's shrill and saucy British media environment. The headline read: "Fornigate."

HEADLINES ABOUT THE CLINTON SCANDALS:
A British Sampler

Sex Scandal in Little Rock: President Fails to Deny 'Six Mistresses' Claim
--Daily Mail, 12/23/93

The Blonde Divorcee Bill Clinton Phoned 18 Times A Day
--The Sun, 12/30/93

A Legend in His Own Bedtime
--Mail on Sunday, 1/2/94

I Fear for My Life, Says Clinton Blonde
--Daily Express, 1/4/94

Clinton Wore My Nightie: Ex-Beauty Queen Tells of Threats to Make Her Keep Quiet Over 'Affair'
--Daily Express, 1/24/94

Clintons' Double Date: Bill Kissed His Girl as Hillary Was Fondled by Lover, Says Aide
--Daily Express, 4/11/94

Fornigate: The Mounting Toll of Clinton's Women
--Sunday Times, 5/1/94

Sidebar H:

The Joke's on Clinton:
A Sampler of Scandal Humor

Most of the press may have been ignoring Troopergate and Paula Jones, but America's late-night comedians found almost as much grist for their humor mills in the sex scandals as in Whitewater. NBC's Jay Leno and CBS's David Letterman cracked a total of 46 jokes about Troopergate and Paula Jones between December 22, 1993 and August 15, 1994. Whitewater generated 52 jokes over the same time period. Until the congressional hearings on Whitewater in the summer of 1994, sex had actually outpaced Whitewater on the late-night comedy rosters. (The hearings may have seemed dull to average viewers, but they were irresistible fodder for comedians.) Incidentally, Leno's humor was consistently more political than Letterman's in both categories, as the chart below shows.

Subject	Total Jokes	Letterman	Leno
Whitewater	52	21	31
Troopergate /Jones	46	18	28
Total	98	39	59

Over time, late-night scandal humor can be as damaging to a public official's image as any front-page headline, as former vice president Dan Quayle would surely agree.

The Best of Whitewater:

On the Clinton Crime Bill's Three Strikes and You're Out Provision:
"With the Whitewater real estate deal and the problems with that Madison Savings and Loan, he's two down right there."

-- Leno, 1/27/94

On the Final Four:
"Not basketball — that's the number of people in the Clinton administration who haven't been subpoenaed yet."

-- Leno, 3/16/94

On the Clintons' $6,000 error in their 1979 taxes:
"When the president does it, it's a discovery. When you do it, it's a felony."

-- Leno, 4/11/94

Hillary Clinton's Top Ten Financial Tips
10) Don't buy furniture--borrow it from the Smithsonian.
9) Raise everybody's taxes--and start grabbing with both hands, Chester!
8) Whatever you do, don't buy land in Arkansas.
7) Three words: extra value meal.
6) Aim scud at Perot, take a billion.
5) Buy low, sell for $100,000.
4) Instead of an expensive name brand stuffing, load your husband up on sawdust.
3) For a quick couple bucks, lease out Socks to a medical testing lab.
2) For a quick couple bucks, lease out Roger to a medical testing lab.
1) Scalp Streisand tickets.

-- Letterman, 3/31/94

On the impact of Whitewater:
"Now, Roger is the Clinton who is being embarrassed by his brother."

-- Letterman, 3/29/94

On Clinton's legal defense fund:
"Earlier today, they received a donation of $1,000 worth of stamps from Dan Rostenkowski."

-- Letterman, 6/29/94

On the Whitewater hearings:
"The three basic questions being raised by the hearings are: What did Clinton know, when did he know it, and who was he dating at the time?"

-- Letterman, 7/28/94

"It's so boring it looks like a bad ad for 'The Hair Club for Men'".

-- Leno, 7/31/94

"Clinton says he's seen none of the hearings. He tried to, but couldn't hear them because of the paper shredder."

-- Leno, 8/4/94

On White House reaction to the defeat of Clinton's crime bill:
"It's good news for Clinton's staff."

-- Leno, 8/11/94

The Best of Troopergate and Paula Jones:

On Arkansas State Troopers' arrest technique:
"O.K. ma'am, you want to step out of the car, put your hands on the governor."

-- Letterman, 12/22/93

On Clinton's naming of a nun to a federal post:
"After all of those Arkansas state trooper allegations, do you get the feeling maybe this was Hillary's choice?"

-- Leno, 2/2/94

On Clinton's message to youths that "sex is not a sport":
"If it was, Clinton would be a lot thinner."
-- Leno, 2/4/94

On Clinton's comment that it was hard to think of brother Roger as a married man:
"I believe it, because, you know, it's hard for the president to think of himself as a married man."
-- Letterman, 3/28/94

On Clinton saying his administration has been the most scrutinized in history:
"Bill, if you're tired of scrutiny, quit dropping your pants."
-- Letterman, 5/13/94

On Clinton's expansion of Head Start:
"Now women in his hotel room will get a 20-minute head start."
-- Leno, 5/19/94

On Clinton urging school kids to practice abstinence:
"That's a little like me urging teens to not break the speed limit, isn't it?"
-- Letterman, 6/6/94

On Clinton's meeting with Queen Elizabeth:
"After all the allegations of extramarital affairs, not paying taxes, these taped phone conversations with alleged lovers, Clinton must have felt like a son to her."
-- Leno, 6/6/94

On news of Wynonna Judd's pregnancy:
"The White House automatically issued a denial."
-- Leno, 5/12/94

On Paula Jones:
> "Clinton always seems to pick women who look like they're afraid their makeup might get stolen, so before they leave the house in the morning they just put on everything they own."
>
> -- Leno, 6/17/94

On Clinton's legal defense fund:
> "He said if there's any money left over, he's going to use it to spend on dates."
>
> -- Letterman, 6/27/94

Top Ten Signs the President Is About to Fire You
> 5) You're an Arkansas State Trooper and you don't know any hot babes.
>
> -- Letterman, 6/28/94

On O.J. Simpson's lawyers' offer of reward money to catch the "real murderer":
> "In an unrelated story, Bill Clinton's lawyers are now offering $600,000 to catch the real womanizer."
>
> -- Leno, 7/20/94

Top Ten Things Heard at President Clinton's High School Reunion:
> 9) President Clinton rubbed up against me. How much do you think I could sue for?
>
> -- Letterman, 7/25/94

On Clinton's television health care advertisements:
> "Have you seen Clinton's health care commercials? He claims it's two minutes a night that can change your life. Isn't that what he promised Paula Jones?"
>
> -- Leno, 8/4/94

GRAPHS AND CHARTS
NOTES FOR ALL CHARTS AND GRAPHS

* Only stories with a substantial focus on a given development in Troopergate, Paula Jones, and Whitewater are counted towards a news outlet's total. Stories with incidental mentions are not included.

* Television, newspaper, and magazine data are for stories appearing between November 1, 1993 and August 15, 1994.

* Magazine statistics include brief stories or update in addition to full-length feature articles. The number of full-length stories appears in a note to Graph #3.

* The tone of network news coverage for key individuals reported in Graph #8 was determined by analyzing individual statements from both news sources and network reporters. "Good Press" is the percentage of explicit positive references; "Bad Press" is the percentage of explicitly negative references. Ambiguous and neutral references were discarded.

* All newspaper and magazine data were gathered using Lexis/Nexis.

* Op-Ed columns and editorials have been omitted from all newspaper statistics.

* All network data were collected by the Center for Media and Public Affairs.

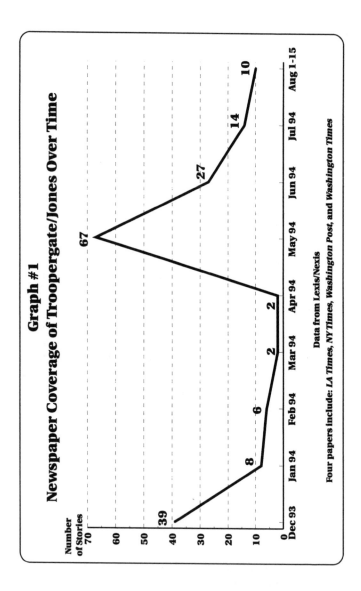

Graph #1
Newspaper Coverage of Troopergate/Jones Over Time

Data from Lexis/Nexis

Four papers include: *LA Times, NY Times, Washington Post, and Washington Times*

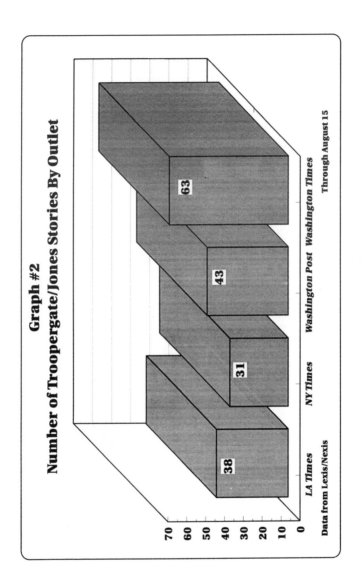

Graph #2

Number of Troopergate/Jones Stories By Outlet

LA Times	NY Times	Washington Post	Washington Times
38	31	43	63

Data from Lexis/Nexis

Through August 15

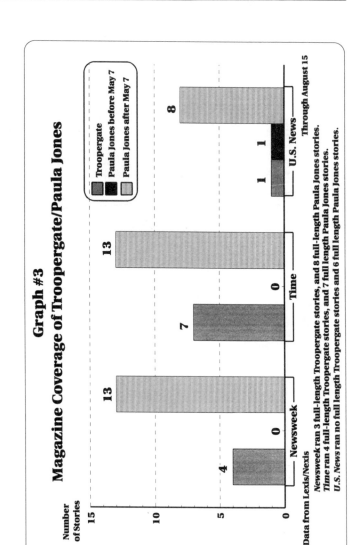

Graph #3
Magazine Coverage of Troopergate/Paula Jones

Number of Stories

Legend:
- Troopergate
- Paula Jones before May 7
- Paula Jones after May 7

Data from Lexis/Nexis

Newsweek ran 3 full-length Troopergate stories, and 8 full-length Paula Jones stories.
Time ran 4 full-length Troopergate stories, and 7 full length Paula Jones stories.
U.S. News ran no full length Troopergate stories and 6 full length Paula Jones stories.

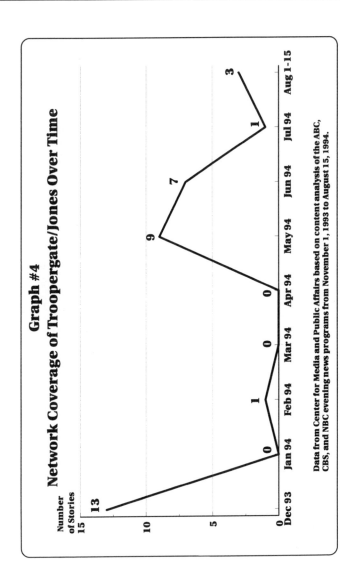

Graph #4

Network Coverage of Troopergate/Jones Over Time

Number
of Stories

Data from Center for Media and Public Affairs based on content analysis of the ABC, CBS, and NBC evening news programs from November 1, 1993 to August 15, 1994.

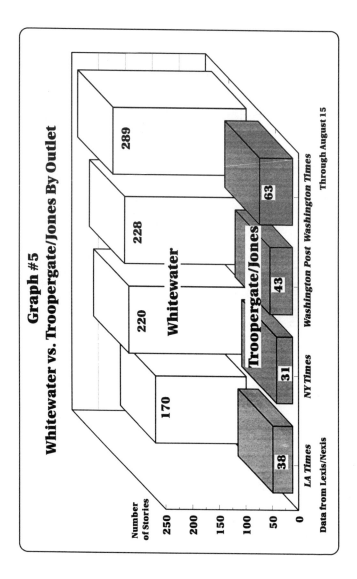

Graph #5
Whitewater vs. Troopergate/Jones By Outlet

Number of Stories

Whitewater

Troopergate/Jones

LA Times — 170 / 38
NY Times — 220 / 31
Washington Post — 228 / 43
Washington Times — 289 / 63

Data from Lexis/Nexis   Through August 15

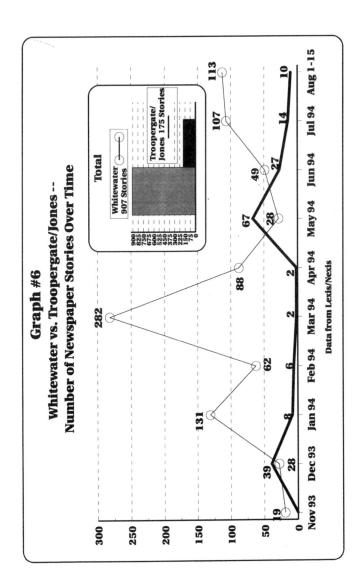

Graph #6

Whitewater vs. Troopergate/Jones --
Number of Newspaper Stories Over Time

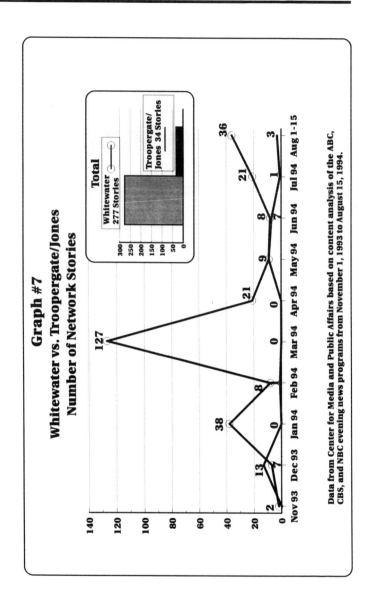

Graph #7
Whitewater vs. Troopergate/Jones
Number of Network Stories

Data from Center for Media and Public Affairs based on content analysis of the ABC, CBS, and NBC evening news programs from November 1, 1993 to August 15, 1994.

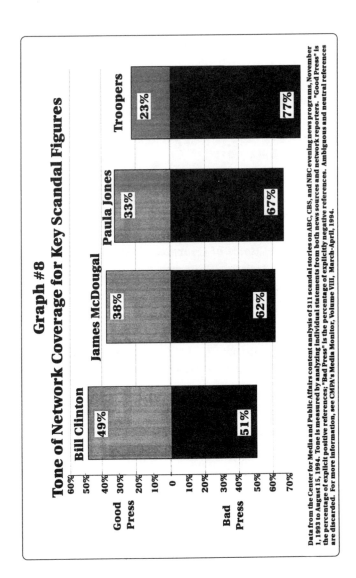

Graph #8
Tone of Network Coverage for Key Scandal Figures

Good Press

Bad Press

Bill Clinton 49% / 51%

James McDougal 38% / 62%

Paula Jones 33% / 67%

Troopers 23% / 77%

Data from the Center for Media and Public Affairs content analysis of 311 scandal stories on ABC, CBS, and NBC evening news programs, November 1, 1993 to August 15, 1994. Tone is measured by analyzing individual statements from both news sources and network reporters. "Good Press" is the percentage of explicit positive references; "Bad Press" is the percentage of explicitly negative references. Ambiguous and neutral references are discarded. For more information, see CMPA's Media Monitor, Volume VIII, March–April, 1994.

Chart # 1

Content of Troopergate Articles
Appearing in Four Papers

	Total	Percent of Stories
Specific Reports of Troopers' Allegations	21	41%
Tactics of Trooper Supporters to Spin Story	7	14
Criticisms of Media Coverage	6	12
Questions of Troopers' Credibility	5	10
Tactics of Clinton Supporters to Spin Story	5	10
Political Effects of Charges	2	4
Polling Statistics Relevent to Troopergate	2	4
Other	3	6

Content of Paula Jones Articles
Appearing in Four Papers

	Total	Percent of Stories
Legal Strategy/Immunity Issue	39	35%
Credibility of Jones/Her Lawyers	24	21
Legal Defense Funds (Clinton and Jones)	20	18
Accusations of Sexual Harassment	13	12
Political Consequences/Politics of Suit	8	7
Hiring of Robert Bennett	6	5
Other	2	2

Note: Percentages may not sum to 100% due to rounding.
Data from Lexis/Nexis   Nov. 1, 1993-Aug. 15, 1994

Chart # 2

Network Coverage - Number of Stories Detailing Various Scandal Allegations

	Total
Whitewater Improprieties	48
Treasury/White House Meetings	43
Sexual Harassment	16
Lying/Misleading Congress	12
Foster Death Investigation	11
Commodities	11
David Hale Loan	9
Document Shredding	7
Troopers' Allegations	5
Other	10

Data from Center for Media and Public Affairs based on content analysis of the ABC, CBS, and NBC evening news programs from November 1, 1993 to August 15, 1994.
Stories may have included discussion of more than one allegation.

Chart # 3

Newspaper Coverage - Number of Stories Detailing Various Scandal Allegations

	Total
Whitewater Improprieties	88
Treasury/White House Meetings	71
Foster Death Investigation	37
Commodities	22
Troopers' Allegations	21
Document Shredding	20
Pressure on RTC Investigators	19
David Hale Loan	15
Sexual Harassment	13
Other	7

Data from Lexis/Nexis   Nov. 1, 1993-Aug. 15, 1994
Stories may have included discussion of more than one allegation.

APPENDIX

List of Interviewees

Name	Title	News Organization	Interview Date**
Fred Barnes	Senior Editor	*The New Republic*	7/20
Gloria Borger	Assistant Managing Editor	*U.S. News & World Report*	7/18
Rita Braver	White House Correspondent	CBS News	7/1
David Brock	Investigative Reporter	*American Spectator*	7/12
Nina Burleigh	Contributor	*Time*	8/2
Chris Bury	Nightline Correspondent	ABC News	7/11
Eleanor Clift	White House Correspondent	*Newsweek*	7/1
Shelby Coffey III	Editor and Executive V.P.	*Los Angeles Times*	9/8*
Francis Coombs	Assistant Managing Editor	*Washington Times*	7/28
Karen DeYoung	Assistant Managing Editor-National News	*Washington Post*	9/8
Greg Ferguson	Former Reporter	*U.S. News & World Report*	7/18
Jeff Gerth	Staff Writer	*New York Times*	7/13
Tom Hannon	Political Director	CNN	8/24
Steve Haworth	V. P. of Public Relations	CNN	9/1
Mark Hosenball	Investigative Reporter	*Newsweek*	7/19
Brit Hume	Chief White House Correspondent	ABC News	6/29
Michael Isikoff	Investigative Reporter	*Newsweek*	7/25
Joe Klein	Contributing Editor	*Newsweek*	7/26
Howard Kurtz	Staff Writer	*Washington Post*	7/11

*Mr. Coffey chose to respond to questions in writing.

**All listed dates are in calendar year 1994.

Name	Title	News Organization	Interview Date**
Sharon LaFraniere	Staff Writer	*Washington Post*	8/5,8/7
Andrea Mitchell	White House Correspondent	NBC News	7/21
Jim Miklaszewski	White House Correspondent	NBC News	8/2
Lisa Myers	Congressional Correspondent	NBC News	7/20
Jack Nelson	Washington Bureau Chief	*Los Angeles Times*	6/30
Scott Pelley	News Correspondent	CBS News	7/27
Harrison (Lee) Rainie	Asst. Managing Editor	*U.S. News & World Report*	9/1
Bill Rempel	Reporter	*Los Angeles Times*	7/14
Tom Rosenstiel	Media Correspondent	*Los Angeles Times*	7/5
Roger Smith	National Editor	*Los Angeles Times*	8/1
Marilyn Thompson	Deputy National Editor for Domestic Coverage	*Washington Post*	8/25
Ed Turner	Executive Vice President	CNN	8/31
Mike von Fremd	Correspondent	ABC News	8/29
Daniel Wattenberg	Investigative Reporter	*American Spectator*	7/21
Bill Wheatley	Vice President, NBC News	NBC	7/21
Michael Wines	White House Staff Writer	*New York Times*	7/6
Jim Wooten	Correspondent	ABC News	7/12

**All listed dates are in calendar year 1994.

THE CENTER FOR MEDIA AND PUBLIC AFFAIRS (CMPA) is a nonpartisan and nonprofit research and educational organization, which conducts scientific studies of news and entertainment media.

During the decade since its formation in 1985, the CMPA has emerged as a unique institution that bridges the gap between academic research and the broader domains of media and public policy. Our goal is to provide an empirical basis for ongoing debates over media fairness and impact through well-documented, timely, and readable studies of media content. Our scientific approach sets us apart from media "watchdog" groups, while our timeliness and outreach sets us apart from traditional academic researchers.

CMPA's primary research tool is content analysis, which is applied to both news coverage and the information content of entertainment messages. We also conduct surveys and focus groups to illuminate the media's role in structuring the public agenda. CMPA studies are frequently featured in news accounts and journalism reviews, as well as in scholarly publications and college textbooks.

The results of CMPA studies are published in *Media Monitor,* the Center's bi-monthly newsletter. To obtain a subscription, or to receive more information about the Center for Media and Public Affairs, please call (202) 223-2942 or write:

**Center for Media
and Public Affairs**
2100 L Street, NW Suite 300
Washington, DC   20037

CMPA STAFF

Dr. S. Robert Lichter
Co-Director

Dr. Linda S. Lichter
Co-Director

John Thomas Sheehan
Executive Director

Daniel Amundson
Research Director

Richard E. Noyes
Political Studies Director

Mary Carroll Gunning
Project Director/Production &
Graphics

Michelle Fernandez
Director of Administration